BOOK SALE

READABILITY CHART

HOW TO USE THIS CHART

Take a pencil or ruler and connect
"Words per Sentence" figure (left)
your
The i
the ce
score.
60.

1.30

1.35

1.40

1.45

1.50

1.55

DATE DUE

WORDS
SENTEN

5 — 5

1.60

.65

.70

10 —

15 —

.75

20 —

25 —

30 —

35 —

.80

52671

.85

.90

.95

00

HOW TO WRITE PLAIN ENGLISH

HOW TO WRITE
PLAIN ENGLISH

A Book for Lawyers and Consumers

Rudolf Flesch

Foreword by Michael Pertschuk
Chairman, Federal Trade Commission

HARPER & ROW, PUBLISHERS
New York, Hagerstown, San Francisco, London

FIRST EDITION

Designer: Eve Kirch

Flesch, Rudolf Franz, 1911–
    How to write plain English.
    Includes index.
    1. English language—Rhetoric. 2. English language—Terms and phrases. 3. Law—Language. I. Title.
PE1479.L3F57   1979   808'.042   76–26225
ISBN 0–06–011278–6

79 80 81 82 83 10 9 8 7 6 5 4 3 2 1

To my grandson Luke

Contents

Foreword

Life treats people unequally. Some barely make it through senior high, or perhaps a few years at a university. Others go to the finest schools of graduate learning and become doctors, lawyers, or college professors. But even for this latter group, there is still hope. They can learn to write Plain English. And in his book, Rudolf Flesch shows us how.

Rudolf Flesch is a man with a vision. And it's a vision to send chills up the spines of lawyers everywhere. Imagine a world in which consumers read insurance contracts and understand them; in which taxpayers leaf through the tax forms and know how much they owe Uncle Sam; in which small businessmen can comprehend the fine print on the red tape. Imagine these things and you will be imagining a world in which lawyers have lost their magic potions. Rudolf Flesch imagines these things, and worse yet, tells us how to make them happen. This book is truly subversive literature.

Some things, however, ought to be subverted, and prime among them is the way we write laws, regulations, and contracts. "Legalese" isn't listed in the foreign language section of any college catalogue, but it probably should be. It takes as long to learn as French or Spanish, and to most people it is just like Greek.

Self-flagellation, though, is not my purpose in writing this foreword. I am, I confess, a lawyer, and a sometime addict to the prose style that Mr. Flesch decries. But with his help I've gone on the wagon, or at least I'm trying, and my colleagues at the Federal Trade Commission are trying with me.

One day last fall I was sailing through what seemed to be a simplified explanation of a proposed FTC regulation governing advertising of home insulation. How nice it would be if the regulation itself were this easy to understand, I thought. It was only then that I discovered that I was reading the regulation itself. It had been "Flesched out." The publisher suggested that I festoon this foreword with similar examples of Rudolf Flesch's good influence on bureaucratic prose. Having read through his book, however, I find it hard to improve on the examples Mr. Flesch has given. In fact, his examples are too good, and too plentiful, and too many have to do with my agency! This is not because the Federal Trade Commission is an especially hardcore perpetrator of bureaucratese. It is rather because over the past few years Mr. Flesch has been devoting particular attention to our linguistic rehabilitation, and is, therefore, especially well acquainted with our crimes against language that made his efforts necessary.

As a consultant, Mr. Flesch has personally helped the dedicated professional staff at the FTC translate a variety of rules, reports, letters, and press releases into Plain English. But his greatest service has been as a teacher and a conscience. Like the comrade from Weight Watchers' Anonymous, his is the little voice we hear over our shoulder when temptation strikes—telling us to avoid fattening our sentences with double negatives or a rambling dependent clause.

The struggle will not be an easy one, and at my agency,

and throughout the government, it has only just begun. Too many educated people still believe, subconsciously perhaps, that a simple sentence betrays a simple mind. In truth, of course, writing Plain English is devilishly hard work, as this book shows us. But it is work that is worthy of the best efforts of our most dedicated and intelligent citizens.

"The great enemy of clear language is insincerity." These are the words of George Orwell, written in 1946. A big government, or a big business that deals with people in terms they cannot readily understand invites suspicion of its motives and disrespect for its goals. Writing Plain English isn't just a matter of cutting down on lawyers' bills or saving a few trees. It is ultimately a matter of restoring people's faith in the institutions of their society. Rudolf Flesch, of course, makes no such grandiose claims for his book. He seeks only to teach us—in methodical, amusing, and clear detail—how to write Plain English. If we can learn to do this, however, we shall be learning how to do a great deal more.

MICHAEL PERTSCHUK
Chairman, Federal Trade Commission

HOW TO WRITE PLAIN ENGLISH

1

Learning Plain English

The Plain English movement officially started on March 23, 1978, when President Carter signed Executive Order 12044. Federal officials, he said, must see to it that each regulation is "written in plain English and understandable to those who must comply with it."

Right away, federal bureaucrats got busy. They appointed committees, assembled task forces and started various Plain English projects.

Actually, Plain English had been slowly making headway even before President Carter sounded his trumpet call. The 1974 Pension Reform Act said that pension plan descriptions for employees must be "written in a manner calculated to be understood by the average plan participant." The 1975 Moss-Magnuson Warranty Act said that warranties of consumer products must be written in "simple and readily understandable language." And some twenty states debated or passed laws calling for Plain English in insurance policies, leases and consumer contracts. Some of those laws defined Plain English by the formula you'll find in this book. Some used other descriptions.

Anyway, there's no longer any doubt that a historic movement is underway. Just as in 1962 the Catholic Church started saying Mass in the vernacular rather than Latin, so there's now a swing of the pendulum from gobbledygook to Plain Engish.

It's not going to happen overnight. It's going to take years, maybe decades, until Plain English will really take hold in legal documents. But if you're a lawyer or a document-drafting bureaucrat, you'd better prepare yourself. Start learning Plain English right now.

But what's there to learn? you say. Everybody knows Plain English. It's the language you've known since childhood. True, you don't use it in writing important documents, but if that's the word from the White House and the state capitols, you'll be glad to oblige. It's just a question of putting down on paper what you've long been familiar with.

Unfortunately, it isn't as easy as that. President Carter may have thought that federal bureaucrats, once shown the error of their ways, would simply drop their poor language habits and go back to Plain English. But he was mistaken. Gobbledygook or legalese is worse than smoking cigarettes. To kick the habit is extremely hard.

So don't kid yourself. If you want to write Plain English, you'll have to learn how. You'll have to study it as if it were Spanish or French. It'll take much work and lots of practice until you've mastered the skill.

I've trained and helped lawyers to write Plain English for some thirty years. Lately, I've been a consultant to the Federal Trade Commission and have worked with its attorneys in drafting consumer notices and regulations. It's difficult but not impossible. And you'll find it fascinating work. This book will show you how it's done.

Before going into details and techniques, I want first to deal with three ground rules. Here they are:

1. Use nothing but Plain English.
2. Know your reader.
3. Use the right tone.

What do I mean by "Use nothing but Plain English"? Well, it's been my experience that lawyers are apt to use Plain English right up to the point where the going gets tough. Then they'll say, This idea is too complex—it can't be put into Plain English, no matter how hard you try. "Plain English," Professor Frank P. Grad of Columbia University Law School said recently, "is a false issue. Many problems that need legislative resolution are complex and difficult. We need complex language to state complex problems of law or fact."

On that theory, you would draft a legal document, and just when the poor layman needed special help in understanding it, you would leave him in the lurch. A classic example is a loan agreement I drafted several years ago for Citibank. By the time it was published, the bank lawyers had gotten hold of my text and changed it drastically. I could hardly believe my eyes when I read this sentence: "To protect you [the bank] if I'll default on this debt to you, I give you what is known as a security interest in my motor vehicle." "Default"? And "what is known as a security interest"? Known to whom? Surely not to the ordinary person who walks into a bank to get a car loan? I'm afraid the language of that loan note should be called "Plain English with spots of mumbo-jumbo."

So—Rule Number One—stick to Plain English through thick and thin. When you come up against a roadblock like *default* or *security interest,* just try a little harder. It's up to you to meet the challenge. Remember that President Carter said it must be "understandable to those who must comply with it."

Now let's have a look at Rule Number Two, "Know your reader."

If you're like most lawyers and bureaucrats, you *don't* know your reader. You do your writing in a vacuum or an air-conditioned ivory tower. This is the way it's always been done, the way you've been taught to do it in college or law school. You try as hard as you can to express your ideas fully and accurately, giving no thought whatever to the poor person who'll have to read and understand what you wrote.

On May 14, 1976—just before I started as a consultant for the Federal Trade Commission—the FTC's so-called "Holder in Due Course" rule went into effect. It said that all consumer credit contracts must carry the following notice (in hard-to-read all-capital letters):

> Any holder of this consumer credit contract is subject to all claims and defenses which the debtor could assert against the seller of goods or services obtained pursuant hereto or with the proceeds hereof. Recovery hereunder by the debtor shall not exceed amounts paid by the debtor hereunder.

This is now the law of the land, and all consumer credit contracts in the U.S. are disfigured by this monstrous clump of legal gobbledygook.

What does it mean? If you're not a lawyer, I'm sure it means absolutely nothing to you. Let me explain:

Back in 1758 there was a case in England called *Miller v. Race.* A promissory note drawn on the Bank of England had been stolen and then sold to an unsuspecting merchant.

The court ruled that the amount of the note must be paid in full. Why? Because if you couldn't rely on the face value of a commercial paper, business couldn't go on.

For two hundred years American courts stuck to this principle, even for papers signed by consumers. If you got a car loan from a finance company and it turned out the car was a lemon and didn't hold up for five minutes on the road, you had to pay your installments to the finance company to the bitter end. Because of *Miller v. Race,* there wasn't a thing you could do.

When the new FTC rule went into effect in 1976, it was a tremendous boon to consumers. Unfortunately, though, they had no way of knowing about it. If they read the new notice on their credit contract, it told them nothing at all.

And did anyone at the FTC foresee this? Were they aware of the fact that nobody but a lawyer could figure out what the notice meant? No, they were not. Their staff report said airily, "While the wording of the notice is legalistic, we believe that it will be understood by most consumers."

Other lawyers and bureaucrats are just as blissfully ignorant of the state of mind of their readers. The Food and Drug Administration in a recent regulation on antacids ruled that certain drug labels must say "Drug Interaction Precautions. Do not take this product if you are presently taking a prescription antibiotic containing any form of tetracycline." How's that for a quick hint to a drugstore shopper?

Or take the people at the Federal Reserve Board. A few years ago they prepared model forms for car and truck leases to consumers. One of the items read "Capitalized Cost Reduction." When I first saw this, I hadn't the slightest idea what it meant. I found the explanation way down on a long list of specific instructions that came with the forms. There the Federal Reserve Board let me in on the secret: "The term 'Capitalized Cost Reduction' is used to indicate a payment in the nature of a downpayment which reduces the value of the leased vehicle to be amortized over the term of the lease." Why didn't they call it a downpayment right there on the form? Obviously because they thought consumers could easily figure out for themselves what was meant by "Capitalized Cost Reduction."

The height of this total alienation from the mass of humanity was reached in 1973 by the lawmakers of my own state of New York. Every retail installment contract, they decreed, must carry notice in at least eight-point type reading as follows:

> NOTICE TO THE BUYER: 1. Do not sign this credit agreement before you read it or if it contains any blank space. 2. You are entitled to a completely filled in copy of the credit agreement.

During the past few years I've seen many New York credit agreements, some of them twenty-inch-long "bedsheets" filled with dense small type, some others stiff cardboard holders with slots for credit cards. All of them end with that touchingly naïve required paragraph. I bet not a single New York consumer ever heeded the advice and read the agreement from A to Z.

All of which, I hope, proves my point that legal document writers don't know who they're writing for. They live in a never-never land where everybody is highly educated and carefully reads every word in every contract, lease or label.

If you still insist that this is true and that people read and understand everything they're supposed to, let me give you a few examples from actual field tests.

Item: In a test of protein supplement labels, 601 people

in the San Francisco area were given a plastic bottle and asked to look at it "just as you would if you noticed it on the shelf at the grocery or health food store and were thinking of buying it." The bottle had a label that said, "Protein supplements are unnecessary for most Americans. The U.S. Public Health Service has determined that the daily diet of most Americans provides adequate protein." The interviewees were then asked whether they saw anything on the bottle that said whether or not people need protein supplements. Seventy-seven percent said no, and 9 percent recalled that it said that people *do* need protein supplements.

Item: In a test of drug ads on TV, viewers were asked whether they remembered the warning "Do not use if presently taking any prescription drug," which had appeared for six seconds at the end of a commercial. Ninety-seven percent couldn't remember. When a voice-over was added to the printed warning, the percentage dropped to 72 percent.

Item: A national sample of 375 people agreed to have an eleven-page "Life Insurance Buyer's Guide" mailed to them, to read it carefully and answer questions about it on the phone. They were paid a silver dollar for their help.

The booklet focused on comparing the cost of different policies. It contained *twice,* in capital letters, the sentence "LOOK FOR THE POLICIES WITH LOW COST INDEX NUMBERS." When asked how one can compare the cost of policies, 69 percent of the recipients couldn't remember anything about index numbers. When reminded of them, 80 percent said they didn't know what they meant.

Item: In a test of commonly used jury instructions, 35 prospective jurors in the Washington, D.C., area were asked to paraphrase them. Each of 14 instructions was twice read to them aloud. The group was well educated. Of the 35 people, 16 had finished college.

One of the instructions said, "A proximate cause of an injury is a cause which, in natural and continuous sequence, produces the injury, and without which the injury wouldn't have occurred." Only one of the 35 people—a man with a Ph.D.—could correctly paraphrase the whole sentence. All the rest misunderstood one or more of the words. Eight thought "proximate" was the same as "*ap*proximate." Five thought they'd heard the phrase "natural cause."

To sum up: Most people don't read legal papers, labels, warnings on TV or what have you. When they do read or listen to such things, they usually don't understand them. If you're writing for "the general public," you'd better remember this basic fact of life.

Since you can't spend several thousand dollars for a field test each time you write something addressed to consumers, I'd recommend that you step out of your office whenever you've finished one of those writing jobs. Find someone in the building who hasn't gone to college. A typist, maybe. Or a maintenance worker. A cafeteria employee. Anyone who qualifies as an ordinary unsophisticated consumer. Let them read what you wrote and tell you what it means. You'll get some surprises.

If you can't find a suitable victim for this kind of mini field test, use your imagination. You must know *somebody* without a college degree. An aunt maybe? A cousin? The meat man at the supermarket? A waitress in your favorite restaurant? Pick your reader or listener and write for him or her.

Finally, if all else fails, I suggest you think of Mrs. Ora Lee Williams. Mrs. Williams was the heroine of the famous Walker-Thomas consumer credit case, which was decided in 1965.

Mrs. Williams lived in a poor section of Washington, D.C. She was "a person of limited education, separated from her husband" and had to support her seven children. Her monthly welfare check was $218. During the years from 1957 to 1962 she bought from the Walker-Thomas Furniture Company "sheets, curtains, rugs, chairs, a chest of drawers, beds, mattresses and a washing machine," adding up to more than $1,800. When the balance was down to $164, she bought a $515 stereo set. Soon afterward she stopped her monthly payments. The company said she'd signed a complex contract that said they could take everything back. The court said Mrs. Williams couldn't possibly have understood that clause and ruled against the company.

Next time you write for consumers, think of Mrs. Williams—poor, semiliterate and not very bright. Do I hear you say that Mrs. Williams is not typical? Of course she isn't, but that's exactly my point. In writing your Plain English piece, *don't* aim at the typical, "average" consumer. That would leave out 50 percent of your readers, those below the average in education, IQ, reading skill or business experience. They need Plain English most. Write for *them*.

And this brings me to Rule Number Three, "Use the right tone." What kind of tone or attitude should you use in writing for Mrs. Williams? Clearly, you should write to her the way you'd talk to her. If she came to your office, you'd ask her to sit down and you'd explain things to her slowly and patiently, making sure she understood each point before you moved on to the next. You wouldn't be stiff and formal. You'd be as friendly and informal as you could be, making her feel that you were sincerely trying to help her.

How does this attitude come through in your writing? By using conversational English, contractions, sentences without verbs, colloquial expressions—the kind of style that looks spoken on the printed page.

For example, let's take the 1977 income tax instructions of the State of Oregon.

In August 1977, Oregon passed a law that said instructions for individual income tax returns must have a Flesch readability score of at least 60. (As I'll explain in the next chapter, this meant that the instructions had to be written in Plain English.) The law was supposed to go into effect in January 1980, but in a burst of enthusiasm they rewrote the tax instructions for the 1977 returns, published in the spring of 1978.

Here are some examples of their style:

You must file an Oregon return if you moved into or out of Oregon during the year and have income subject to Oregon tax. But you can't use the forms in this packet.

An audit is a review of a return to make sure it was prepared according to tax law. It's protection for all taxpayers to make sure that everybody pays their share of taxes.

You would include interest from State of Washington bonds or from San Francisco city bonds. You'd leave out interest from Oregon bonds.

Line 3. *Occupation.* Fill in what you do for a living.

Need more time to pay? See p. 7.

Still can't find the number? Contact your county clerk or local public school.

You see how friendly and pleasant this is? If you write for ordinary taxpayers or consumers, you simply *have to* learn to write *can't* and *it's* and an occasional *you'd.* You'll have to learn to write, "Need more time to pay?" because that's the way it flows into the typewriter if you're really attuned to your audience.

What about grammar? Well, you'll have to forget the stiff, 19th-century grammar you probably learned in school. Don't hesitate to write, "Everybody pays their share." That idiom has been used by good writers since 1526. Fielding wrote, "Everybody in the house were in their beds."

And what about slang? You may have had a slight nervous tremor when you came across "Contact your county clerk." If so, relax. *Contact* as a verb has been in literary usage since 1927 and is now fully accepted. The same is probably true of most words you shy away from in writing because you think they're slang. Nine times out of ten they're perfectly good English. Anyway, you can't be prissy about "slang" or "bad grammar" and write effective instructions for taxpayers or notices to consumers.

To bring home the point and give you a good insight into how this kind of translation works, here are two before-and-after examples taken from the Oregon tax instructions. First, a paragraph from the old 1976 instructions:

Deceased persons. A return must be made by the executor or administrator of the decedent's estate or by the surviving spouse or other person charged with the care of the property of the deceased. If the surviving spouse or next of kin desires to claim the refund, an affidavit should be submitted with the return. This affidavit (Form 243) is available at all Oregon Department of Revenue district offices, or it can be obtained by writing the Oregon Department of Revenue, State Office Building, Salem, Oregon 97310.

In the 1977 instructions, the corresponding paragraph read like this:

My husband died last year. Can I file for him? Yes. The husband or wife of someone who dies, or the legal representative must file the return. Use the form the person would have used if living. If you claim a refund, attach Form 243 to show you have a right to the deceased person's refund. Write for Form 243 to: Oregon Department of Revenue, Salem, Oregon 97310, or pick it up at any of our district offices.

Here's another paragraph as it appeared in the 1976 instructions:

Minors. If you are a minor, you are required to report your income and deductions on your own return and not on the return of your parents. However, any tax attributable to a minor's income from personal services, if not paid by the minor, is considered assessed against the parent by reason of parental rights.

Here's the 1977 version:

Do I have to report money my children earned? Your children have to report income and deductions on their own returns, not on yours. But if they don't pay their taxes, it's up to you to pay them.

One question that is sometimes raised with such materials is that the tone is patronizing or "talking down." For example, there was some criticism of that sort when we put a simplified consumer notice in the FTC hearing aid rule. Customers had to be given a notice that they could return a hearing aid, with a cancellation notice, within 30 days. The notice said:

Take the notice to our office or have it postmarked by _____.

Ask for a receipt if you bring us the notice yourself. If you mail us the notice, send it "certified mail, return receipt requested." Be sure you get to the Post Office before closing time on the last day of the 30-day period.

I remember exactly why I used this language. I did it because the FTC 1972 Door-to-Door Sales regulation, in a similar notice, said this:

> To cancel this transaction, mail or deliver a signed and dated copy of this cancellation notice or any other written notice, or send a telegram to _____ at _____ not later than midnight of _____.

This is the kind of thing you'll never write if you keep your addressee—Mrs. Williams—firmly in mind. Mrs. Williams, I'm afraid, would be apt to take this literally and drop her cancellation notice into a nearby mailbox five minutes to midnight on the last day. Then, if the company says she missed the deadline, she'll be out of luck. Far better to instruct people to be businesslike and send an important notice "certified mail, return receipt requested" before the post office closes for the day. If this is "patronizing," O.K.

For a different type of problem in hitting the right tone, let's take a letter I rewrote for the FTC. It was addressed to home insulation contractors. Under the law, the commission could send out a letter to a company that hadn't done anything unfair or deceptive but might do so in the future. This so-called "Section 205" letter gave those firms the exact details of certain earlier decisions so that they would know exactly what to avoid to stay within the law. The standard form letter read like this:

> Dear _____:
> On January 4, 1975, the Federal Trade Commission Act was amended to provide that a person, partnership or corporation is liable for civil penalties of $10,000 per vio-

lation for engaging in acts or practices which the Commission has determined to be deceptive or unfair in a prior cease and desist proceeding with actual knowledge that such act or practice is unfair or deceptive and is unlawful under Sec. 5(a)(1) of the Federal Trade Commission Act [15 U.S.C. 45(m)(1)(B)]. A copy of the relevant statutory provisions is attached.

This letter together with the enclosed Federal Trade Commission decisions and a synopsis of those decisions is to inform you of certain practices which the Commission has found unlawful under Section 5(a)(1) of the Federal Trade Commission Act and to notify you of the potential liability of _____ for civil penalties under the above described statutory provisions if _____ is, in fact, engaged in those practices.

In order to avert possible action by the Federal Trade Commission for civil penalties of $10,000 per violation you should immediately ensure that you are not engaged in any of the practices proscribed by the enclosed decisions.

Please contact [attorney's name] of this office [phone number] if you have any questions regarding the applicable law or your possible liabilities.

Sincerely,

The FTC attorney who asked me to lend a hand said the letter was unsuccessful. People didn't read it. It came with several hundred pages of case decisions and usually landed in the wastebasket. Could I draft something more effective?

I drafted a nice, informal letter. It was a little too friendly for the attorney's taste, and he wrote, "I admit my initial reaction was extremely negative. However, on second thought, I understand your objective. . . . I very much like the tone of your letter." He came back with the following compromise, hitting, I think, exactly the right tone:

Dear _____.

Under the law, you and your firm may be subject to civil penalties of up to $10,000 or more if you engage in certain unfair or deceptive practices. The purpose of this letter is to inform you of the acts and practices the Federal Trade Commission has found to be deceptive or unfair, and to notify you of the potential liability of _____ for civil penalties if _____ is in fact engaged in these practices.

I apologize for sending you such a bulky package of papers. I'm required to do this to make sure you know of the Federal Trade Commission decisions that are important to you and your firm. This material, as difficult and bulky as it may be, is important and must be read carefully. You should then check to be sure that you or your firm are not engaged in any of the practices prohibited by these decisions.

If you need any help with this material, or if you have any questions, please do not hesitate to call (name and phone number) or come by our offices at _____.

> Sincerely,

And that's how the "Section 205" letter went out. I am sure the changed tone saved many of those letters from the instant wastebasket treatment.

Now let's look at what can be done about the letter of the law itself. As I said, I collaborated with the FTC lawyers on over a dozen new regulations.

At first, I suggested—out of habit, I guess—my friendly, casual contractions and other conversational features. But after a while I discovered that for actual legal documents this didn't work. I got some inkling of this problem when an insurance policy I'd rewritten had to be labeled with a little box that said, "This is your policy. Keep it in a safe place."

Why? Because the agents promptly mistook it for an explanatory brochure.

Then there was the argument about the apartment lease. I had rewritten that document with an introductory sentence that said, "You agree to follow the rules below" and then followed it up with "Do's and Don'ts" like "Don't keep any pets" and "Don't sublet the apartment." But the lawyer I worked with said this couldn't be done. He painstakingly rewrote the whole lease, starting each section with "You agree to" do this and "You agree to" do that. Otherwise, he said, it would sound too offhand and casual and a judge might say it wasn't binding.

When I drafted my first regulation with the FTC attorneys, I ran into the same problem. You can't make it too warm and friendly, they said. The businessmen who'll have to live by those rules must know the government means business. Be serious and *sound* serious. Instead of "don't" say "do not." Instead of "it's illegal" say "it is unlawful."

For instance, here are some before-and-after examples from the FTC hearing aid rule.

The original proposed regulation had said:

> *"Used hearing aid."* A hearing aid which has been worn for any period of time by a buyer or potential buyer; *Provided however,* That a hearing aid shall not be considered "used" merely because it has been worn by a buyer or potential buyer as part of a bona fide evaluation conducted to determine whether to select that particular hearing aid for that buyer, if such evaluation has been conducted in the presence of the seller or a hearing aid health professional selected by the seller to assist the buyer in making such a determination.

In the Plain English version this was changed to:

> A hearing aid is used if it has been worn for any length of time. This includes new hearing aids that

have been returned. However, if a hearing aid was only tried on in front of a salesperson or professional, it is still new.

Again, the old regulation had said:

> No seller shall make any representation to members of the consuming public without clearly and conspicuously disclosing that it is a seller of hearing aids. The disclosure requirement of sec. 440.8(a) will be satisfied by a clear and conspicuous statement of the name of the seller's business, if that name includes the words "hearing aid center" or other words which clearly identify that the establishment is a seller of hearing aids.

In Plain English this became:

> *Say you are a seller.*
> In all signs, ads, and other written materials, clearly and conspicuously explain that you sell hearing aids. If your firm's name clearly refers to hearing aid sales, using its name will serve this purpose. Also, when you start to talk to potential customers, make sure they understand that you sell hearing aids.

The old regulation had said:

> No seller shall represent that it is a governmental or other public service establishment or a nonprofit medical, educational or research institution unless such is the fact. Such a representation is made by the use of names such as "hearing center" (but not "hearing aid center"), "hearing institute," "hearing aid institute," "hearing bureau," "hearing aid bureau," "hearing clinic," "hearing aid clinic," "speech and hearing center," "speech and hearing aid center," and "senior citizen surveys."

The Plain English regulation said:

> Do not use a name that says or implies that your

firm is something it is not. If you are in business for profit, your name must not say or imply that you are a nonprofit group or service, or a government or educational agency, or that you do public service or research. Do not call your firm an "institute" unless it regularly does research or teaching. Do not call it a "bureau" if it is not a government agency. Do not call it a "clinic" if it does not regularly offer medical services supervised by a physician. Do not call it a "hearing and speech center," "speech and hearing center," "speech and hearing aid center," or any similar name if it does not regularly offer hearing services supervised by a physician or audiologist.

The old regulation had said:

> No seller shall prepare, approve, fund, disseminate or cause the dissemination of any advertisement which, because of its form and/or content, cannot be easily understood as being designed to effect the sale of hearing aids, or to create interest in the purchase of hearing aids, by the audience to whom such advertisement is directed.

The Plain English regulation said:

> *Ads that do not look like ads.*
> Make sure that your ads do not look like something else, such as news items or public service announcements.

Quite a difference, isn't it? And this was done without contractions, without conversational features, just plain straightforward English.

The FTC hearing aid rule was the first federal regulation written in Plain English. (An earlier attempt by the Federal Communications Commission didn't quite come off.) It proved, once and for all, that legal documents can be written that way.

But it shows even more. If you look at these four examples, you'll see that there is not only a difference in style but there are also many minor changes that clarify what is said, make it sharper, more specific, and—a point lawyers are interested in—more enforceable. Why is this so? Because, in the process of rewriting the regulation in Plain English, the two attorneys and I had to take the proposed regulation completely apart, analyze the meaning of every word and put each idea under a microscope.

I'll always remember one final session we had, lasting from 9 A.M. to 6 P.M. on a hot summer day. Once more the three of us went over every word and every comma. "What does this mean?" I'd ask them innumerable times, and they'd explain, give examples, tell me how the section came about and what it was supposed to do. And then we'd change it to say what we wanted it to say in the plainest, clearest, most exact words we could find.

I'm still proud of that first Plain English regulation. It's not only crystal clear and fully understandable, but it reads well.

In other words, it's not only Plain English but *good* English.

2

Let's Start With the Formula

If you want to learn how to write Plain English, you must learn how to use a readability formula.

Of course this isn't true if you have a talent for writing. I've come across quite a few people who can write a booklet explaining an insurance policy simply because they have the knack. But I take it you're not blessed with that knack. You belong to the 98 or 99 percent of mankind who must learn Plain English the hard way. If so, you must know where you are and where you want to go. You need a yardstick, a measuring tool, something against which you can check your progress. That's what a formula is for.

There are by now dozens of readability formulas in existence, but for general use there are only a handful to choose from. They fall into two groups—those based on sentence length and a word *list* and those based on sentence length and word *length*.

I worked out my own formula because I tried to apply the word list formulas to adult reading matter and got nowhere. So I went in a new direction and constructed a formula based on word *length* rather than a list. It was the first of this type and has become the most widely used formula in the country. There are other sentence and word length formulas, all of which are variations of mine. Their results aren't much different from my formula but, I think, mine is easier to use. So what you're going to get in this chapter is a mini-course in using the Flesch formula.

I developed the formula in the early 1940s. It measures the average sentence length in words and the average word length in syllables. You put these two numbers into an equation and get a number between 0 and 100 that shows you the difficulty of your piece of writing. If it's too hard to read for your audience, you shorten the words and sentences until you get the score you want.

At first blush you may think this is a very crude way of dealing with writing. Writing means conveying ideas from one mind to another. To use a mechanical gadget for this doesn't seem like an intelligent approach.

But wait a minute. I spent several years of my life doing the underlying research for this formula and got my Columbia University Ph.D. degree for it. I can assure you that it is based on some very complicated facts of human psychology. It works because it is based on the way the human mind works.

When you read a passage, your eyes and mind focus on successive points on the page. Each time this happens, you form a tentative judgment of what the words mean *up to that point.* Only when you get to a major punctuation mark—a period, a colon, a paragraph break—does your mind stop for a split second, sum up what it has taken in so far, and arrive at a final meaning of the sentence or paragraph. The longer the sentence, the more ideas your mind has to hold in suspense until its final decision on what all the words mean *together*. Longer sentences are more likely to be complex—more subordinate clauses, more prepositional phrases and so on. That means more mental work for the reader. So the longer a sentence, the harder it is to read.

Exactly the same thing is true of words. Some words are short and simple, others are long and complex. The complexity shows up in the prefixes and suffixes. *Take* is a simple, short word that doesn't present much difficulty to a reader. But *unmistakably* has the prefixes *un-* and *mis-* and the suffixes *-able* and *-ly* and gives the mind much more to think about than *take*. (My *very* first readability formula was based on a count of prefixes and suffixes to measure word complexity. A few years later I tried to make it easier to use and changed to a count of syllables. Statistically, the results are about the same.)

In using the formula, you count words and syllables to measure the mental work the reader will have to do. A paragraph that measures 0 on the scale is apt to give the reader a headache; a paragraph that scores 100 is child's play.

Let's take an example. Take the sentence "John loves Mary." That's short and sweet and obviously presents no reading difficulties. Its score is 92, which means "very easy."

Now let's say the same thing with a little more sophistication—"John has a profound affection for Mary." This adds some complexity to the idea. It rates "Plain English"—a score of 67—but gives the reader a little to think about. Just exactly what *are* John's feelings toward Mary?

Now let's go into further complexities: "Even though John is not normally given to a display of his deeper emotions, he allegedly has developed a profound affection for Mary, as compared to the more equable feelings he seems to have for Lucy, Fran and, to a lesser extent, Sue." This has a score of 32 ("difficult") and throws the whole affair into a state of some obscurity and ambivalence. The sentence now compares in difficulty with the *Harvard Law Review.*

All right, I've given you the fundamentals. Here's how you use the formula:

Test only the running text of your piece of writing. Skip titles, headings, subheads, section and paragraph numbers, captions, date lines and signature lines.

Step 1. Count the words.

Count the words in your piece of writing. Count as single words contractions, hyphenated words, abbreviations, figures, symbols and their combinations, e.g., *wouldn't, full-length, TV, 17, &, $15, 7%.*

Step 2. Count the syllables.

Count the syllables in your piece of writing. Count the syllables in words as they are pronounced. Count abbreviations, figures, symbols and their combinations as one-syllable words. If a word has two accepted pronunciations, use the one with fewer syllables. If in doubt, check a dictionary.

Step 3. Count the sentences.

Count the sentences in your piece of writing. Count as a sentence each full unit of speech marked off by a period, colon, semicolon, dash, question mark or exclamation point. Disregard paragraph breaks, colons, semicolons, dashes or initial capitals *within* a sentence. For instance, count the following as a single sentence:

You qualify if—
(1) You are at least 58 years old; and
(2) Your total household income is under $5,000.

Step 4. Figure the average number of syllables per word.

Divide the number of syllables by the number of words.

Step 5. Figure the average number of words per sentence.

Divide the number of words by the number of sentences.

Step 6. Find your readability score.

Find the average sentence length and word length of your piece of writing on the chart on page 25. Take a straightedge or ruler and connect the two figures. The intersection of the straightedge or ruler with the center column shows your readability score.

You can also use this formula:

Multiply the average sentence length by 1.015. Multiply the average word length by 84.6. Add the two numbers. Subtract this sum from 206.835. The balance is your readability score.

The scale shows scores from 0 to 100. Zero means practically unreadable and 100 means extremely easy. The minimum score for Plain English is 60, or about 20 words per sentence and 1½ syllables per word. Conversational English for consumers should score at least 80, or about 15 words per sentence and 1⅓ syllables per word.

All Plain English examples in this book score at least 60.

READABILITY CHART

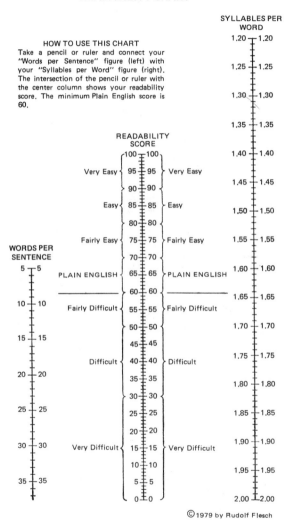

SYLLABLES PER WORD

HOW TO USE THIS CHART
Take a pencil or ruler and connect your "Words per Sentence" figure (left) with your "Syllables per Word" figure (right). The intersection of the pencil or ruler with the center column shows your readability score. The minimum Plain English score is 60.

READABILITY SCORE

Very Easy

Easy

Fairly Easy

WORDS PER SENTENCE

PLAIN ENGLISH

Fairly Difficult

Difficult

Very Difficult

© 1979 by Rudolf Flesch

Here are the scores of some reading materials I've tested. These are average scores of random samples.

Comics	92
Consumer ads in magazines	82
Movie Screen	75
Seventeen	67
Reader's Digest	65
Sports Illustrated	63
New York Daily News	60
Atlantic Monthly	57
Time	52
Newsweek	50
Wall Street Journal	43
Harvard Business Review	43
New York Times	39
New York Review of Books	35
Harvard Law Review	32
Standard auto insurance policy	10
Internal Revenue Code	minus 6

Here's how the scores translate into school grades. Reading matter with the score shown on the left side will be easy for students on the level shown on the right.

Score	School Level
90 to 100	5th grade
80 to 90	6th grade
70 to 80	7th grade
60 to 70	8th and 9th grade
50 to 60	10th to 12th grade (high school)
30 to 50	college
0 to 30	college graduate

Next, let me give you two important tips.

First, if you want to rewrite a passage to get a higher score, you'll have to cut the average sentence length. This means you'll have to break up long, complex sentences and change them to two, three or four shorter ones. In other words, sprinkle periods over your piece of writing. When you're turning subordinate clauses into independent sentences, you'll find that a lot of them will start with *And, But* or *Or*. Don't let that bother you. It's perfectly good English and has been good usage for many centuries. The Old Testament says, "And God said, Let there be light; and there was light." The New Testament says, "But Jesus gave him no answer." And Mark Twain wrote, "Man is the only animal that blushes. Or needs to." So never mind that old superstition. And don't—please don't—put unnecessary commas after your *And's, But's* and *Or's*.

Second tip: When it comes to replacing complex words with simple ones, take first aim at words with prefixes and suffixes, like *establishment, available* or *required*. Often the best Plain English replacement is a two-word combination like *setting up, in stock* or *called for*. If you can't think of a good substitute, use any good thesaurus or book of synonyms. You'll find that there's no complex, legalistic word that can't be translated into Plain English.

Now let's have a little practice session. Here's the first sentence of the warranty that came with a TV set I bought a few years ago. I'll call the company Pixon.

> Pixon warrants to the original consumer purchaser that it will replace Pixon parts, transistors and tubes in this Pixon color television receiver with new or rebuilt Pixon parts, transistors and tubes or at its option repair any such Pixon part, transistor or tube in this receiver which, after regular installation and normal use shall be found to have been defective and which is returned to an authorized Pixon dealer within one year from the date of original consumer purchase of the receiver.

To find the readability score, let's count the words and the syllables. There's no need to count sentences because it's all one sentence. It has 83 words and 1.66 syllables per word. This gives us a score of minus 18. This score means "hopelessly unreadable," well below the average score of the Internal Revenue Code. Sentences with 83 words are virtually impossible to read and understand instantly. You have to reread them several times and carefully analyze what they say.

If you do this, you'll find there are eight different ideas packed into this sentence. If you break it up and use one sentence for each separate idea, you wind up with eight sentences.

There are all kinds of hidden clauses and conditions. The warranty protects only the first buyer. The company has the right to give you used, rebuilt parts as replacements. Or they can give you no replacements at all if they want to, and just repair the set. The set must be "found" to have been defective (by whom?) and must be returned to the store. This means you'll have to lug it there—no pickup. (The famous "Baldwin piano clause.") Also it says the warranty is for one year only.

All right, let's rewrite the stuff, splitting up the sentence and using such simple words as *set* instead of *receiver* and *buyer* instead of *purchaser*. If this was a longer passage, we'd insert two or three subheads to make it easier to read. As it is, a few paragraph breaks will do. Here we go:

> This is a 1-year warranty for parts, transistors and tubes. It starts the day you buy your set.
>
> You're protected only if you're the first buyer. Your set must have been properly installed and normally used.
>
> To get service, take the set to one of our authorized dealers. We'll replace any defective parts, transistors and tubes. Instead of new parts, we may use rebuilt parts as replacements. Or we may repair the defective parts and put them back in your set.

This has a total of 81 words. The average sentence length is 10 words, the average word length is 1.38 syllables. The readability score is 80—the easy, conversational style you should use for consumers. (I put in some conversational touches like *you're* and *we'll*.) This is the style level you find in consumer ads in mass-circulation magazines. It's just right for such things as consumer notices or warranties.

Also, this kind of writing plays fair with the reader, in contrast to the original 83-word sentence with its many hidden traps and conditions.

Now let's look at something else. This comes from an FTC case against a supermarket chain I'll call Plazamart. The company had advertised specials in the local papers and then didn't mark the advertised prices on the shelves. So an FTC lawyer and a company lawyer prepared an agreement in which the company promised to do certain things. Among them were posters they'd put up in their stores. The posters would show a copy of the ad and a notice to the customers that they should check the advertised prices.

The first notice the two lawyers came up with read as follows:

All items advertised are required by law to be sold at prices no higher than the advertised prices in each Plazamart store, except as specifically noted in this ad. If you have any questions, the store manager will be glad to assist you.

In order to avoid overcharging that might result from incorrect price marking, Plazamart asks each of its customers to inspect the price marked on each item he or she selects to insure that such price is correct, and report instances of merchandise being marked with an incorrect price to store personnel. Plazamart is legally obligated to make available any advertised item at the advertised price during the applicable advertised sale periods regardless of the price marked on any unit of the advertised item. (In the case of coupon offers you must, of course, present the appropriate coupon, or make the minimum purchase in order to receive the advertised price.)

If any checker, when confronted by you with the fact that he is about to ring up, or he has rung up, an advertised item at a price higher than the advertised price, refuses to correct the error immediately or to ring up the item at the advertised price, the customer is requested to report the incident to the store manager.

This is unbelievably bad writing. Here are two grownup people, expensively trained lawyers, who seriously plan to put this 213-word-long notice on posters in supermarkets. Didn't they see, in their mind's eye, the harassed housewife, with her full shopping cart, stopping to laboriously read the notice? It takes an average person about a minute to read 200 words of ordinary prose, and maybe three minutes to read 200 words of legalistic gobbledygook—if they can decipher it at all. This notice has average sentences of 36 words and average words of 1.57 syllables. Its readability score is 37, just a little easier than the *Harvard Law Review.* Can you see Mrs. Customer standing there for a solid three minutes, studying the poster?

And what does she read? She reads *are required to* instead of *must, assist* instead of *help, incorrect* instead of *wrong, inspect* instead of *check, selects* instead of *picks* or *buys . . . personnel . . . obligated . . . available . . .* a whole collection of formal, bureaucratic words. Instead of giving the checker the coupon, she's asked to *present* the *appropriate* coupon (what else?). Instead of being charged, she will *receive the advertised price* (a refund?). Instead of talking to the checker, she will *confront* him (and cross-examine, maybe?). Finally, she's *requested to report the incident* (in triplicate?).

When a new FTC attorney came into the case, he decided to try his hand at Plain English. He came up with this:

Notice to Our Customers
To assure correct charging of advertised prices, please check the price of any advertised item you purchase against the price indicated in our ad and report any errors to store personnel. If errors are not corrected to your satisfaction, please advise the store manager.

Well, the man tried. He threw out all unnecessary verbiage and got the notice from 213 words down to 44. There are now only two sentences with an average length of 22 words. The average word has 1.66 syllables and the readability score is 44—up from the *Harvard Law Review* level to the *Wall Street Journal* level.

But that's still not good enough for the rushed and tired shopper. It still is full of *purchase, indicated, personnel* and the business jargon word *advise* in the sense of *tell.*

The attorney realized this and asked me to simplify the notice further. My final version was this:

To Our Customers
Please check the price of each advertised item you buy against the price in our ad. If it's more, ask the checker to charge only the price in the ad.

If there's any problem, please let me know. Thank you.

The Manager

You see what I did? I said *please* twice and *thank you* once. I said *it's* and *there's.* I let *The Manager* sign—at least by putting *The Manager* at the end. In other words, I tried to write something the shopper could read and understand in a jiffy *and* the company would agree to. (I saw no point in hinting to the public that the company had misbehaved and had to correct illegal price markings.)

Oh yes. The total number of words in this final version was 40, the average sentence length 10 words and the average word length 1.20 syllables. The readability score was 95, easier than comics or magazine ads. After all, as I keep explaining to my lawyer friends at the FTC, those consumer notices compete with highly skilled, super-Plain English ad copy. If we want to tell things to consumers, we'd better learn to speak their language.

3

Oceans of Verbiage

The most legalistic FTC regulation I worked on was one on mobile homes. The man who originally wrote it must have been a true devotee of archaic gobbledygook. His draft teemed with *hereinbelow, notwithstanding, set forth therein, alleged, purported, pursuant to, as aforesaid, then and in that event, forthwith, above-described* and *with respect thereto.* In one unforgettable phrase, he wrote of "defects which have been determined to deleteriously affect the health and safety of the occupants of mobile homes containing such defects." In another place he wrote, "Such a visit and review shall be immediately initiated by the manufacturer upon receipt of an unreasonable number of meritorious complaints or unsatisfactory reports, questionnaires or other similar communications from consumers."

When I had finished the first draft of my simplified version, I saw that it was very much shorter than the original.

I wrote a memo to the new attorney on the job and asked
her to check whether I'd left out anything. The answer was
no. I had covered exactly the same territory. All the words
I had left out were unnecessary.

I counted the words in the original regulation and those
in my Plain English version. The original had 4,782 and
mine had 2,292. I had cut the verbiage by 52 percent.

Let me give you an example. One of the original sections
read this way:

Prohibited conditions precedent

In connection with the manufacture, sale, offering for
sale, distribution, and service of mobile homes produced
or sold primarily for use by consumers in commerce, as
"commerce" is defined in the Federal Trade Commission
Act, it is an unfair or deceptive act or practice within the
meaning of section 5 of that Act, notwithstanding the provisions of section 441.4(g), for any warrantor of a mobile
home to:

(a) disseminate a written warranty or any documents
associated therewith which require or purport to require
the return of any home or any defective part thereof to
the location of its manufacture as a condition precedent
to obtaining warranty repairs or service;

(b) disseminate a written warranty or any documents
associated therewith which require or purport to require
the return of a warranty card, owner's registration card,
or any similar document bearing certain information about
the consumer or the retail purchase transaction as a condition precedent to the manufacturer's obligation to perform warranty repairs and service on said consumer's
mobile home.

This section has 166 words. The first paragraph has 67.
Is it needed? No. Let me explain why.

The FTC operates under the FTC act. The act says the
agency can issue regulations "which define with specificity

acts or practices which are unfair or deceptive acts or practices in or affecting commerce." When I started as a consultant to the agency, the usual procedure was to preface *each section* of each regulation with a paragraph that showed this legal basis. The first thing I did in simplifying those regulations was to consolidate all those repetitious paragraphs and put them up in front as section 1. My typical opening was this:

Section 1. *What this regulation does.*

This regulation deals with . . . in or affecting "commerce" as defined in the Federal Trade Commission Act. If you are covered by this regulation and break any of its rules, it is an unfair or deceptive act or practice under section 5 of that Act.

I did the same with the mobile home rule and got rid of a dozen repetitious paragraphs with one fell swoop.

Now let's look at the rest of the section.

"Disseminate." Why did the writer use the word *disseminate?* Because he wanted to use one long word instead of three short ones—*give or offer.* If you count the syllables, you'll find that *disseminate* has four syllables and *give or offer* also has four syllables. The gain in brevity is zero. And it throws the heavy word *disseminate* into the reader's path. He'll have to figure out whether *disseminate* here possibly means something the ordinary words *give or offer* don't mean. He'll find that it doesn't.

Next, "a written warranty." Why use the word *written?* No reason. The whole regulation deals with written warranties only. It says so in several places. Nobody could conceivably doubt that spoken warranties are not covered.

Next, "or any documents associated therewith." Well, of course a warranty might consist of two pieces of paper, one labeled "warranty" and the other labeled something else.

Would this open a possible loophole for shady operators? Surely not.

This is the point where some lawyers start arguing. You never can tell, they say. There may be some judge somewhere—I call him Judge Fiendish—who'll rule against you on this kind of technicality. You have to draft legal documents in such a way that no Judge Fiendish will be able to trip you up.

I don't believe in this argument. Whenever I asked my lawyer friends in private industry—the drafters of bank loan notes and insurance policies—they assured me that most judges are biased against corporations. Then, when I asked the same question of my lawyer friends in the government, they said with equal conviction that most judges are biased against consumers.

Let's forget about Judge Fiendish. Let's write so that no reasonable person will misinterpret what we're trying to say. Let's change "a written warranty or any documents associated therewith" to "a warranty."

Next, "which require or purport to require." Again, is this necessary? What would be the situation covered by "purport to require"? Well, maybe a particularly nasty warranty might say something like "Repairs can only be performed at our factory in Anchorage, Alaska." Would Judge Fiendish say this is O.K.? I don't believe it. Let's make it "require."

Next, "the return of the home or any defective part thereof." Sheer verbiage. Let's change it to "return of a home or part." (If it wasn't defective, there would be no need for warranty service.)

Next, "to the location of manufacture." Means "to the plant."

Next, "as a condition precedent." What is a condition precedent? Webster's Unabridged Dictionary explains that there are two complementary legal terms—"condition precedent" and "condition subsequent." "Condition precedent" means "a condition whose fulfillment must precede the taking effect of a contract." "Condition subsequent" means "a condition whose fulfillment invalidates a contract previously in effect (as when a horse is bought on condition that he prove sound)."

Now why did our hero of "hereinbelow" and "deleteriously affect" say "condition precedent"? Because he couldn't help it. The two phrases "condition precedent" and "condition subsequent" were so firmly implanted in his mind that he had to say "condition precedent" even where it was wholly unnecessary. Of course, *all* conditions of a warranty are "conditions precedent"—conditions you must fulfill *before* the warrantor will give you service. Otherwise, if the warranty contained a "condition subsequent"—let's say that you must pay for installing new parts—the serviceman could come to your house, put a replacement tube in your TV set and then rip it out again if you didn't pay him for his labor.

So let's just say "condition." Let's say "get" instead of "obtain." Let's drop "repairs" since they're included in "service." Let's simply say "as a condition for getting service."

The third paragraph starts with a lot of repetitious words. Then follows "a warranty card, owner's registration card, or any similar document bearing certain information about the consumer or the retail purchase transaction." Sheer verbiage. It simply means "any kind of warranty card."

Finally, there's the peroration—"the manufacturer's obligation to perform warranty repairs and service on said consumer's mobile home." The last five words are wholly unnecessary. Why refer once more to "said consumer"?

Could anyone—even Judge Fiendish—suddenly think of the Millers of Idaho instead of the Smiths of Kentucky? And do we need still another reference to a mobile home? We're not talking about pianos, are we?

After I'd studied the proposed regulation with its bloated language, I read the staff report that explained it. It said:

> Section 441.6 of the proposed rule forbids the dissemination of warranty documents which contain clauses which represent: (a) that it is necessary to return the defective home, or part thereof, to the factory, or (b) that it is necessary to return a "Warranty Registration Card" or similar document in order to secure warranty repairs.

Still legalese, but only 52 words instead of 166.

And what would the section be in Plain English? Here's what I suggested:

Forbidden Conditions

There are two conditions for getting service that you must never put in a warranty:

(a) You must not ask consumers to ship a home or part back to your plant.

(b) You must not ask them to mail you any kind of warranty card.

What I've described in these last few pages is simple, garden-variety editing. The point is that usually this isn't done with legal prose. The legal fraternity has convinced the rest of us that all those legalistic words and phrases are absolutely necessary to make a document legally valid. Mustn't touch. If you change "hereinbelow" to "later," it'll cost the client—or the government—untold thousands of dollars. Legal language is sacrosanct.

Nonsense. Ask any good lawyer and he'll tell you it's all a myth. Or read Professor David Mellinkoff's classic book

The Language of the Law. He takes 109 pages to make hash of the whole argument.

Professor Mellinkoff also goes into great detail on the subject of "terms of art" or "words of art." There are only a handful of those technical terms, he says, that are indispensable for talk among lawyers. He mentions, for instance, *certiorari, ex parte, dictum, habeus corpus, laches, mandamus, res judicata, stare decisis.* As you see, most of those terms are Latin.

But even these genuine terms of art must be explained if they're used in writing for laymen. The other day a friend of mine showed me her will, which had recently been drawn up by her lawyer. She asked me what the phrase "per stirpes" meant. I explained that it means "by branches of the family." But I thought, Why didn't her lawyer explain this to her? Did he think she was fluent in Latin?

Or take another example. Look at a warranty you may have around. If you're like most adult Americans, you have a cache somewhere, filled to the brim with warranties for your car, your TV set, your camera, your toaster, your vacuum cleaner and your automatic pencil sharpener. Look through them and you'll find that each has some reference to "implied warranties" and "consequential damages." Are these terms explained? Of course they aren't.

Some time ago the FTC put out a flyer on warranties. It says:

> *Implied warranties.* "Implied warranties" are rights created by state law, not by the company. All states have them.
>
> The most common implied warranty is the "warranty of merchantability." This means that the seller promises that the product you buy is fit for the ordinary uses of the product. For example, a reclining

chair must recline; a toaster must toast. If it doesn't, you have a legal right to get your money back.

Later on the flyer says:

Consequential damages. Normally, your warranty rights include the right to "consequential damages." This means the company must not only fix the defective product, but must also pay for any damage the product did. If your freezer breaks down and the food in it spoils, the company must pay for the food you lost.

That flyer is an excellent model of how to deal with "terms of art" when you're writing for laymen.

Then there are the famous legal doublets—*aid and abet, cease and desist, let or hindrance, null and void* and dozens more. They go back to 1066 and the Norman conquest, when lawyers hit upon the bright idea of coupling French and Anglo-Saxon words, just to make sure everybody knew what was meant. By now these expressions are quaint little relics of bygone times. They don't fit into a 20th-century legal document, but give it a nice antique flavor.

There wouldn't be any harm in this—except for the waste of paper—if our modern lawyers hadn't taken this innocent device and made it into something entirely different. They've fallen into the habit of using not only doublets but triplets, quadruplets, quintuplets and so on. Each time they're stumped and can't find the right word, they simply write a string of almost-right words, hoping that at least one of them will fit the situation at hand.

You don't believe me? I assure you that this is now a routine way of drafting legal documents.

For instance, take this section, which I found in a proposed protein-supplement FTC regulation:

Inconsistent and derogating representations
No representation shall be made which, directly or by
implication, *contradicts, negates* or *is inconsistent with*
any disclosure required or described by any provision of
this part, or in any way *obscures, mitigates* or *derogates
from* the intent or meaning of such disclosure.

What does this mean? Well, the writer wanted to make
sure the prescribed warning labels wouldn't be made use-
less by the supplement seller. What's the use of warning labels that say protein supplements are worthless or even
dangerous if right there on the shelf is a big picture of Muhammad Ali stuffing himself with protein supplements?

When the writer couldn't find the exact words to describe such underhanded shenanigans, he used the shotgun
principle. Let's put in—let's see now—*contradicts, negates,
is inconsistent with, obscures, mitigates* and *derogates.* Between them these six words surely will cover everything.

But they don't. *Inconsistent with* is pretty wide and perhaps will cover the Muhammad Ali picture, though nobody
knows what Judge Fiendish would say to that. *Contradicts?*
Maybe. *Negates?* Too narrow. *Obscures?* Too vague. *Mitigates?* A poor fit. *Derogates from?* What does that word
mean anyhow?

What the regulation writer should have done, of course,
is what any professional writer would have done to begin
with. He should have used those standard writer's tools—
the dictionary, the thesaurus or the book of synonyms. By
looking up the six words in the dictionary, he'd have
learned very quickly that not one of them is the exact word
needed here. None of them describes exactly all the sneaky,
tricky ways in which a clever dealer might try to make a
mockery out of a government regulation.

The problem can be properly solved only by taking some
time with a thesaurus or book of synonyms. There the

searcher would have found at least four words to fill the bill—*subvert, sabotage, undermine* and *undercut.*

You'll notice that two of these words are right on target but unfortunately not Plain English—*subvert* and *sabotage.* One of the other two—*undercut*—may be considered slang by some people. This leaves us with the good, plain, exactly right word *undermine.* Let's use it to rewrite the section:

Do not undermine warnings.

This rule calls for warnings on labels and in ads. Do not undermine them in any way.

Don't think that that shotgun blast of six poorly chosen words is an all-time record. Just the other day I came across a string of *nine* near-synonyms. I found it in a proposed FTC regulation on prescription eyeglasses. Here it is:

It is an unfair act or practice for any person to engage in any activity which has the effect of *prohibiting, hindering, restricting, reducing, burdening, altering, limiting, changing* or *impairing* the dissemination of information pertaining to the sale or offer for sale of ophthalmic goods or services.

What were those nine verbs supposed to mean? Well, the FTC had found that prices of eyeglasses varied tremendously. In Cleveland the same bifocals cost $28 in one store and $43 in another. In New Jersey the same pair of eyeglasses ranged from $16 to $55. In Tulsa prices for the same item varied from $22 to $37.50.

Why was this so? Largely because many states banned advertising of eyeglasses and virtually all opticians' and optometrists' associations did the same. Since the associations couldn't make laws, they did the next best thing and struck off their lists all opticians and optometrists who advertised. The expelled members were made to suffer in various ways.

To cover such indirect pressure tactics, the regulation writer felt he needed those nine verbs. Do they fit? No. The first three—*prohibit, hinder* and *restrict*—are too narrow. *Reduce* is too wide. *Burden* is unclear. *Alter* means something different. *Limit*—again too wide. *Change* and *impair* don't fit at all.

Again, let's hunt through thesauruses and synonym books. There are at least five words that fit the indirect pressure tactics of the professional associations. They are *inhibit, stifle, discourage, deter from* and *prevent.*

If we want a Plain English word, *inhibit* and *deter from* are clearly out of the running. *Prevent* doesn't have enough of that blacklisting, blackmailing flavor. This leaves *stifle* and *discourage. Stifle* is shorter, but *discourage* describes more exactly what the associations are up to. Let's say *discourage:*

It is an unfair act or practice for anyone to discourage ads for eyeglasses.

4

The Indispensable "You"

August 25 marks the anniversary of a great day for the Plain English movement. On that day in 1976 the Federal Register carried a notice of an FTC proceeding. Up to that date those notices had always been written in stiff legalese without the slightest trace of ordinary human discourse, let alone courtesy.

This notice was different. The third paragraph, addressed to "interested persons," started with—lo and behold—the word *Please.* It said:

> Please send data, views and arguments on any issue of fact, law or policy that may have some bearing on the proposed rule. Your comments need not be limited to the designated issues listed in Section D. You may comment on any aspect of the proposed rule. Any earlier comments you may have sent have been placed in the public record and need not be sent again.

This almost unheard-of bit of Plain English in the Federal Register was the result of my rewriting the standard notice that had been used by the FTC. It certainly is easier to read than the original. The corresponding paragraph of that version had been:

> All interested persons are hereby notified that they may continue to submit written data, views and arguments on any issue of fact, law, policy and discretion which may have some bearing upon the proposed rule. The scope of these written comments is not restricted to the designated issues, set forth below. Comments previously submitted in response to the Initial Notice have been placed in the public record and need not be resubmitted.

This is stiff and impersonal. As you can see, the main difference between the two versions is the "you" approach. Once the reader is addressed directly and personally, it's natural to unbend and be as straightforward as you'd be in face-to-face conversation.

I consider the "you" style as absolutely indispensable for Plain English. In fact, in my first readability formula, I used a count of personal pronouns, including *you,* as a third element in addition to the length of sentences and words. Later I simplified the formula but the pronoun *you* is just as important for readability as it ever was.

In his book *The Language and the Law,* Professor David Mellinkoff shows that all legal documents were originally letters. In the Middle Ages legal documents started out with the salutation "Greetings." A reminder of those formal openings is the phrase "Know all men by these presents."

So it makes a great deal of sense to start legal documents with a salutation. The bank loan notes and insurance policies I rewrote all start with the name and address of the customer or policyholder. The loan notes carry the salutation "Dear Customer." The text of the document then flows naturally, calling the customer "you" and referring to the bank or insurance company as "we." Once this is done, the direct, Plain English style is firmly set.

I also used "you" in the regulations I rewrote for the FTC. The difference between that approach and the old-style impersonal legalese was striking. Here are a few examples.

The original version of the FTC home insulation rule said:

> Any advertisement which compares the effectiveness or savings resulting from the advertised insulation to one or more other types of insulation shall base the comparison on equal coverage areas for the product being compared; and in addition to the disclosures about the advertiser's product required in paragraph (a) above, the advertiser shall disclose the R-value of the insulation to which the advertised product is being compared.

Now let's look at the Plain English version addressed to "you."

> If your ad compares one type of insulation to another, the comparison must be based on the same coverage areas. You must give the R-value at a specific thickness and the coverage area of each insulation. You also must give the statement explaining R-values. If you give the price per square foot, you do not have to give the coverage area.

See the difference? A typical small businessman would have no trouble understanding it, but would have been put off by the sheer weight of the verbiage the thing was wrapped in before.

In writing those regulations, I tried to focus on a typical small businessman rather than a semiliterate consumer like

Mrs. Williams. My choice for a living, known person to write to was a roofing contractor who recently did some work on my house. He's a young man, still under thirty. I'll call him Jack Andrews. I never saw him in anything else than blue jeans and heavy work boots. He has shoulder-length blond hair and is very intelligent and competent at his job. The thing I remember is that he gave me his estimate on a slip of paper he ripped out of his notebook. I don't think he's much of a reader, but he would certainly try to cope with a bank loan agreement or a government regulation. The trouble is he couldn't possibly read and understand those documents as they're usually written today.

Now let's look at something from another FTC regulation. This is from the funeral rule. Here is a paragraph from the original version:

It is an unfair or deceptive act or practice for any funeral industry member to discourage a customer's purchase of any funeral merchandise or service which is advertised or offered for sale, with the purpose of encouraging the purchase of additional or more expensive merchandise or services, by:

(i) disparaging its quality or appearance, except that true factual statements concerning features, design, or construction do not constitute disparagement;

(ii) misrepresenting its availability or any delay involved in obtaining it;

(iii) displaying or otherwise offering for sale broken, soiled, or defective merchandise;

(iv) suggesting directly or by implication that a customer's concern for price or expressed interest in inexpensive funeral merchandise or services is improper, inappropriate, or indicative of diminished respect or affection for the deceased.

You can see for yourself the steady march of repetitions, the reference to what "constitutes disparagement," the use of the synonyms "improper" and "inappropriate," and the telltale use of the words "is indicative of" instead of the simple word "shows."

Here is what the passage looks like in the "you" style:

> Do not discourage customers from buying goods or services you offer or advertise. Do not downgrade their quality or looks; but you can make true factual statements about them. Do not mislead customers about whether or how soon they can get those items. Do not offer or display broken, soiled or damaged goods. Do not suggest or imply that concern for price or interest in low-cost goods or services shows little love or respect for the person who died.

I felt a sense of accomplishment when I'd written this paragraph. I still think it's good English. The "you" allowed me to write a fluent, unified paragraph that gave funeral directors, I hope, a clear notion of what they should avoid. I even managed to sneak the word *love* into a government regulation.

Now to my final example. This is from the FTC used-car rule. I had no hand in writing it. The attorney in charge got interested in the Plain English project, started rewriting his regulation in the "you" style and wound up with a Plain English version that needed no further editing.

Here's the original version of a section on window stickers:

> In connection with the offering for sale, sale or distribution of any used motor vehicle to the public, in or affecting commerce as "commerce" is defined in the Federal Trade Commission Act, as amended, it is an unfair or deceptive act or practice for any used motor vehicle dealer to fail to affix to the right rear window of any used motor vehicle offered for sale a disclosure statement containing

the following information in the order it appears below and in a clear and conspicuous manner.

The attorney told me he'd disliked this style to begin with. He said that once he started with "you" he was carried along by the simple, direct style he'd embarked on and the regulation practically wrote itself. No trouble at all.

Here's his version of the window sticker section:

Before you offer a used vehicle for sale to a consumer, you must prepare, fully fill in and display on that vehicle a form just like the form shown below. Use a side window to display the form so someone outside the vehicle can read it. You can remove a form temporarily from the window during any test drive, but you have to put the form back on the window as soon as the test drive is over.

In each of those FTC regulations the attorneys were careful to define "you." The insulation rule says, "You are covered by this regulation if you are a member of the home insulation industry." The funeral rule says, "You are covered by this regulation if you are in the business of selling funeral goods or services to the public." And the used-car rule says, " 'You' means any dealer, or agent or employee of a dealer."

So, if you feel you have to define the meaning of "you" for your document, by all means do so. But there's one basic rule. Whatever you are writing—a loan note, insurance policy or government regulation—make "you" the person who must comply with it or sign it. Several years ago, when I wrote a simplified loan agreement for Citibank, I made the mistake of calling the customer "I" and the bank "you." (Somehow I thought that the signer of a note should also be its apparent author.) I was quite wrong in this. It made the real authors of the note—the bank lawyers—pretend they were writing in the name of the customer. This made the whole note sound phony.

Unfortunately Citibank was quickly imitated by other banks. The other day I got a mailing piece from Chase Manhattan Bank. It offered a loan agreement referring to the customer as "I" and the bank as "you." One sentence said:

> If I have at any time given you a security interest in any of my property under any General Security Agreement, Collateral Promissory Note or other similar agreement, the security in such property (other than stock, which you expressly agree does not secure my debts to you under this agreement) may, also, secure my debts to you under this agreement.

This is *not* the kind of sentence Jack Andrews, the roofer, would ever write. Chase Manhattan tried to write Plain English but failed miserably.

I'm afraid their lawyers just don't have the knack.

5

How to Write Plain Math

One of the most confusing words in the English language is the word *whichever.* You've seen it often. "Whichever is larger." "Whichever is less." Or, as a rather unfeeling husband put it in a will that figured in a recent court case, "My wife Jane shall receive the income from the trust until she dies or remarries, whichever occurs first."

What is the meaning of the word *whichever*? According to Webster's Unabridged Dictionary, it is "no matter which one," as for example in the sentence "I would like to speak to your father or mother, whichever is at home." In other words, *whichever* stands for "it makes no difference which."

But the way the word is used in legal documents, it doesn't mean that at all. The poor widow of the man who made that will doesn't have a simple choice between dying and remarrying. What her husband tried to do—and successfully did, even though his phrasing was rather brutal—was to give her the trust income for life, but cut it off if she married again.

So the legal *whichever* does *not* mean "no matter which." Rather, it means a cutoff point. The phrase "whichever is larger" means a lower cutoff point or minimum. "Whichever is less" means an upper cutoff point or maximum. I know this sounds paradoxical, but that's the way it is. Let me repeat: The words "whichever is greater, larger, more" fix a minimum and mean "at least." The phrase "whichever is less" fixes a maximum and means "up to."

For instance, a bank loan note says, "Borrower is required to pay a late charge of 5% of any installment past due for 10 days or $5.00, whichever is less." This means "If you are over 10 days late in paying an installment, you must pay a late charge of 5%, but only up to $5."

On the other hand, a state income tax instruction says, "The allowable standard deduction is (a) $525, or (b) 13% of federal adjusted gross income, whichever is larger." This means "You can take a standard deduction of 13% of your federal adjusted gross income, or at least $525."

Let's go on to some other features of legal math. Lawyers never put any bit of arithmetic the way everybody is used to seeing it. Instead, they turn it upside down and make everything as difficult as possible.

Here, for example, is section 6657 of the Internal Revenue Code.

Bad Checks

If any check or money order in payment of any amount receivable under this title is not duly paid, in addition to any other penalties provided by law, there shall be paid as a penalty by the person who tendered such check, upon notice and demand by the Secretary, in the same manner as tax, an amount equal to 1 percent of the amount of such check, except that if the amount of such check is less than $500, the penalty under this section shall be $5 or the amount of such check, whichever is the lesser.

At first glance, this looks like the "whichever is less" bit, but if you look a little closer, you'll find that there is more to it. The penalty is 1%, so for a bad check of $500 you have to pay $5. But what if the bad check itself is under $5—say $2.50? Then, the law says, your penalty is the amount of the check itself.

Let's translate:

If you try to pay your taxes with a bad check, you must pay a special penalty, on top of all the other penalties fixed by law. IRS has to send you a demand notice. The penalty is 1% of the bad check, but at least $5. If the bad check was under $5, it's the amount of the check.

Of course this sample from the tax code is just child's play. Let's try something a little harder. Section 3(24) of the 1974 Pension Reform Act says:

The term "normal retirement age" means the earlier of—
(A) the time a plan participant attains normal retirement age under the plan, or
(B) the later of—
(i) The time a plan participant attains age 65, or
(ii) the 10th anniversary of the time a plan participant commenced participation in the plan.

This neat combination of "the earlier of" and "the later of" is the kind of thing that'll give most people a stinging headache. Let's sort it out. Here's what we get:

Your plan must fix a normal retirement age. That age must not be over 65, except for those who joined when they were over 55. For them, the normal retirement age must be fixed at 10 years after they joined.

If your plan fixes an earlier normal retirement age—say 60 or 62—it must make the same exception for those who joined less than 10 years before.

How do you handle a more elaborate piece of arithmetic? Let's take for example section 4062(b) of the Pension Reform Act. This has to do with a pension plan that runs out of money. The law has set up a government insurance corporation that pays the missing pensions to the employees. But the employer must pay the government back. How much? When this part of the law was debated in the Senate, it was decided to limit this liability. The report said, "The employer's contingent liability is limited to 100 percent of the loss up to 30 percent of his net worth."

After the Senators had settled that point, they called in the legal staff and told them to draw up a proper section of the law. Here's what the staff lawyers came up with:

> Any employer to which this section applies shall be liable to the corporation in an amount equal to the lesser of—
>
> (1) the excess of—
>
> (A) the current value of the plan's benefits guaranteed under this title on the date of termination over
>
> (B) the current value of the plan's assets allocable to such benefits on the date of termination, or
>
> (2) 30 percent of the net worth of the employer.

It isn't every section of the law that contains such an immortal phrase as "in an amount equal to the lesser of the excess of." Let's get to work and simplify it.

By far the best way to handle this kind of thing is to break it into steps and write them down in one-two-three order. Like this:

To figure out what you owe the corporation, do this:

Step 1. Figure the current value of the guaranteed benefits.

Step 2. Figure the current value of the assets from which these benefits must be paid.

Step 3. Subtract the assets (Step 2) from the benefits (Step 1). The balance is the total loss of the plan.

Step 4. Figure your net worth.

Step 5. Multiply this figure by .30.

You owe the corporation the total loss (Step 3), but only up to 30% of your net worth (Step 5).

You see what this does? As long as you take the reader by the hand and guide him through numbered steps, you can't possibly go wrong.

That's about all I have to say about legal math. It's ridiculously simple. Use "up to," "at least" and numbered steps and you'll have solved those seemingly unsolvable writing problems. After all, those sections contain nothing but ordinary grade school math. Adding, subtracting, multiplying, and here and there a simple fraction. There are no quadratic equations, no calculus, no imaginary numbers. Why make it impenetrable?

I would stop here, but I can't resist the temptation to show you the worst piece of legal math I ever found. It's section 2523(a) of the Internal Revenue Code:

Gift to Spouse

(1) Where a donor who is a citizen or resident transfers during the calendar quarter by gift an interest in property to a donee who at the time of the gift is the donor's spouse, there shall be allowed as a deduction in computing taxable gifts for the calendar quarter an amount with respect to such interest equal to its value.

(2) The aggregate of the deduction allowed under paragraph (1) for any calendar quarter shall not exceed the sum of—

    (A) $100,000 reduced (but not below zero) by the aggregate of the deductions allowed under this section for preceding calendar quarters beginning after December 31, 1976; plus

    (B) 50 percent of the lesser of—

        (i) the amount of the deductions allowable under paragraph (1) for such calendar quarter (determined without regard to this paragraph); or

        (ii) the amount (if any) by which the aggregate of the amounts determined under clause (i) for the calendar quarter and for each preceding calendar quarter beginning after December 31, 1976, exceeds $200,000.

I won't pretend that I was able to puzzle this out by myself. I looked it up in a textbook on taxation. Here is what I found:

You have to pay only half the gift tax rate for gifts to your wife or husband, but this is arranged in a peculiar way. For the first $100,000 of such gifts during your lifetime you pay no gift tax at all. For the next $100,000 you pay the full gift tax. After that you pay 50 percent. So if you're filthy rich and give your wife millions of dollars worth of gifts, your total gift tax is cut in half. But if you're so poor you can give her only a measly $100,000 or even less, you get a free ride—gifttaxwise, that is.

That's clear enough, but I owe it to you to rewrite the section in Plain English. Here goes:

Gift to wife or husband.

This section applies only to U.S. citizens and residents and only to gifts made after December 31, 1976.

If you give any property to your wife or husband, you must pay gift tax as follows:

(1) There is no tax on gifts up to a lifetime total of $100,000.

(2) On the next $100,000 you must pay the full tax.

(3) After that you pay 50%.

6

Wonderland of Definitions

The word *buyer,* according to the dictionary, means "one who buys." But, according to the FTC eyeglass rule, it means "any person who has had an eye examination."

What's the reason for this? Why do lawyers use those weird definitions? Let me explain.

Once upon a time a lawyer lost a lawsuit because of a mistake he'd made in drafting a document. He'd used a word that could be interpreted in two different ways and the judge—Judge Fiendish, no doubt—had ruled against him. So the lawyer swore he'd never make that kind of mistake again. He'd define all key words in all his documents so there would never be the slightest doubt of what was meant. He did so, and other lawyers followed his example. Soon the method caught on. Today there's hardly a contract or regulation that doesn't start with a string of definitions. It's routine. Everybody does it. That's the way it's taught in law school, and that's the way to protect your client or agency.

But that routine opened the door to a lot of mischief. Lawyers loved their new freedom from the dictionary. If you can redefine each word you use, you no longer have to search for the right word that'll say exactly what you mean. It's a cinch. Use any word that happens to be handy and explain, in a section called "Definitions," that it means such-and-such.

In Chapter 3 I said that lawyers, in contrast to professional writers, rarely bother to find the right word. Instead, they often write down a string of *almost right* words, hoping that one of them will fit. Another way to solve the problem is by definitions. Use a word that's *clearly wrong* and then define it to fit.

The definition of a buyer as "anyone who has had an eye examination" is a good example. The main purpose of the FTC eyeglass rule was to encourage price advertising. But while the FTC lawyers were at it, they also thought of giving consumers a chance to have their eyes examined, get a prescription and then go elsewhere to get it filled cheaply. Eye doctors and optometrists don't like this. They treat eye examinations as part of the sale of glasses. They don't want customers to walk out of their offices and go elsewhere to buy their glasses. So the FTC lawyers put in their regulation that doctors and optometrists can't refuse to give customers their prescriptions. This is what they wrote:

> In connection with the performance of eye examinations, it is an unfair act or practice for a refractionist to fail to give to the buyer a copy of the buyer's prescription immediately after the eye examination is completed.

Then someone noticed that the word *buyer* didn't quite fit. A smart optometrist might figure out that people who have their eyes examined are not yet "buyers." By deliberately misinterpreting the rule he might get out from under it. And who knows, some Judge Fiendish might agree with him. What to do? A professional writer would do the obvious thing and rewrite the passage without using the word *buyer*. For instance, he might simply write:

> You must give patients a copy of their prescription as soon as you have finished the examination.

But lawyers are not professional writers. When faced with this kind of problem, they'd never think of using the word *patient*. Instead, they'll redefine a *buyer* as someone who's had an eye examination.

This misuse of definitions is now common in legal drafting. When the FTC funeral rule was being prepared, one section of it read:

> It is an unfair or deceptive act or practice for any funeral service industry member, whose establishment contains one or more casket selection rooms, to fail to display therein the three least expensive caskets offered for sale for use in adult funeral services, in the same general manner as other caskets are displayed, *Provided,* That if fewer than twelve (12) caskets are displayed, only one of the three least expensive caskets must be displayed.

At a hearing a witness said the section should be changed to include smaller funeral homes who used manufacturers' showrooms or catalogs. The FTC lawyers agreed. But did they rewrite the section? Of course not. They simply struck out the reference to showrooms and added this definition of *display* in the definitions section:

> To "display" is to show customers funeral merchandise which is offered for sale without special ordering, in a selection room maintained by the funeral service indus-

try member, a manufacturer, a wholesaler, a supplier, or any combination thereof, or by other means such as photographs or catalogs.

Obviously this definition is wrong. The dictionary meaning of *display* is "to put or spread out so as to be seen." To make *display* mean the use of photographs or catalogs is wholly misleading.

In my own redraft of the FTC funeral rule I didn't use a definitions section. Instead, I changed the section about showing inexpensive coffins to this:

You must display the three least expensive adults' caskets you offer just like all others. If you display less than 12 adults' caskets, you must include *the* least expensive one you offer.

This applies to any display of caskets you offer without special ordering. It may be in your own showroom or that of a manufacturer, wholesaler or supplier. The rule also applies if you use photographs or catalogs.

A third example of a misused definition comes from the original FTC mobile home rule, which I mentioned in Chapter 3. This one is a beaut.

The main purpose of the mobile home rule was to set deadlines for repairs under a warranty. Customers had complained that they were left high and dry in their new homes for weeks or months if something went wrong that had to be fixed under the warranty. So the regulation said that emergency repairs had to start within three days and others within seven days—"in the normal course of business." And what did "in the normal course of business" mean? It was defined like this:

"Normal course of business" refers to the usual or regular manner of operation of the business enterprise in question under ordinary conditions. "Normal course of business" does not include:

(1) Conditions under which abnormal demands are made upon service capabilities as the result of natural disasters, or other acts of God or the government, or any other event beyond the control of the warrantor and, where applicable, its authorized dealers or other third parties which places an unusually large demand upon service facilities; and

(2) Events such as disasters, strikes, acts of the government, instances of force majeure or other occurrences which are beyond the control of the warrantor or, where applicable, its authorized dealers or other third parties, which prevent the warrantor and, where applicable, its authorized dealers and other third parties from responding to service requests within the time periods stated herein; and

(3) Slight omissions or deviations from the provisions of this part which are inadvertent, unintentional, and are not due to bad faith.

When I read this the first time, I was utterly confused. I simply couldn't see the difference between paragraph (1) and paragraph (2). Then I studied it more closely and found that paragraph (1) refers to situations that cause "abnormal demands upon service capabilities"—or "an unusually large demand upon service facilities," you take your pick—while paragraph (2) deals with situations that prevent the warrantor from "responding to requests within the time periods stated herein." The first list includes disasters, "acts of God or the government," and other events. The second list again includes disasters and acts of the government, but also includes strikes and "force majeure"—which means exactly the same as "act of God."

And then there's paragraph (3), which adds to all those strikes, disasters and catastrophes "slight omissions or deviations" like not-quite-matching paint or having to come back to put a missing knob on a door.

Anyway, it's a splendid example of the ultimate in definitions. When I rewrote the regulation in Plain English, I didn't use any definitions, of course. Instead, I put in the following brief section:

> *Events beyond your control.* You have a valid excuse for missing those repair deadlines if disasters, strikes, acts of the government or similar events beyond your control put abnormal demands on your services or keep you from meeting the deadlines. The same goes for your service agents.
>
> You are also excused from meeting the deadlines in case of slight delays or oversights, as long as you acted in good faith.

And now let's turn to insurance policies. They are notorious for using endless, vastly complicated definitions of *everything.* If you have a car or homeowners insurance policy handy, look at it. You'll find that most of the coverage of the policy is buried in a definition of "the insured" that runs for hundreds of words. No, pardon me—it's a definition of "the Insured" with a capital *I.* Why? Because insurance companies have fallen into the habit of marking all those specially defined words with a capital initial. You say you didn't know that? Well, the insurance people don't care. They've done their bit to warn each policyholder that he should read the definitions.

I looked up my own automobile policy to find a sample definition. (I'll call the company the Protective Insurance Company.) This is how they define a "hit-and-run automobile":

> **The term "hit-and-run automobile" means an automobile which causes bodily injury to the Insured arising**

out of physical contact of such automobile with the Insured or with an automobile which the Insured is occupying at the time of the accident, provided:

(a) there cannot be ascertained the identity of either
the operator or the owner of such a "hit-and-run automobile";

(b) the Insured or someone on his behalf shall have reported the accident within 24 hours or as soon as
reasonably possible to the police, peace or judicial officer or to the Commissioner of Motor Vehicles, and shall
have filed with Protective within 90 days thereafter a
statement under oath that the Insured or his legal representative has a cause of action arising out of such accident for damages against a person or persons whose
identity is unascertainable, and setting forth the facts in
support thereof; and

(c) at the request of Protective, the Insured or his legal
representative makes available for inspection the automobile which the Insured was occupying at the time of the
accident.

You see what this does? A "hit-and-run" driver, according to the dictionary, is one "who does not stop after being
involved in an accident." But, as far as the Protective Insurance Company is concerned, that definition doesn't
mean a thing. According to *them,* a "hit-and-run automobile" is one only if you, the victim, report the accident to
the police within 24 hours *and* give Protective a sworn affidavit within 90 days *and* let them inspect your car. Otherwise that other car that hit yours and then vanished forever
isn't a hit-and-run car at all. To Protective it's just a phan-
tom and they won't pay you a cent.

But wait a minute. While I had my insurance policy out,
I looked a little farther and found *another* definition of
"hit-and-run" on page 7. (The first one appeared on page
4.) Here it is:

"Hit-and-run automobile" means a motor vehicle which causes bodily injury to an Insured arising out of physical contact of such automobile with the Insured or with an automobile which the Insured is occupying at the time of the accident, provided:

(a) there cannot be ascertained the identity of either the operator or owner of such "hit-and-run automobile";

(b) the Insured or someone on his behalf shall have reported the accident within 24 hours to a police, peace or judicial officer or to the Department of Motor Vehicles in the state where the accident occurred, and shall have filed with Protective within 30 days after the accident a statement under oath that the Insured or his legal representative has a cause or causes of action arising out of such accident for damages against a person or persons whose identity is unascertainable, and setting forth the facts in support thereof; and

(c) at Protective's request, the Insured or his legal representative makes available for inspection the automobile which the Insured was occupying, if so, at the time of the accident.

I put both definitions of "hit-and-run" in this book because this will show you how extremely difficult it is to study a lengthy legal paragraph and remember everything in it. At first blush, you surely thought the definitions were the same. At least, that's what I thought at first. But I took the trouble to compare them word for word. My little detective work paid off. The two definitions are not the same at all, and my insurance isn't as good as I thought it was.

What I found is this. The first definition on page 4 was in Section II, Part I, called "New York Automobile Accident Indemnification Coverage." (I live in the state of New York.) Under that definition I must report a hit-and-run accident to the police within 24 hours "or as soon as reasonably possible." Then I have 90 days to file my affidavit with Protective.

The second definition appears on page 7 in Section II, Part II, called "Out of State Uninsured Motorists Insurance." That definition says again that I must report the accident to the police within 24 hours. But it does *not* say "or as soon as reasonably possible." And it gives me only 30 days—not 90—to file my affidavit with the company.

There are also other differences. The first definition says "90 days thereafter," apparently meaning 90 days after making the report to the local police. But the second definition says "30 days after the accident," which is different. Also, near the end, the second definition says "the automobile which the Insured was occupying, *if so.*" In the first definition the words *if so* are missing. In fact, that's a proper correction since the hit-and-run clause covers not only a collision of two cars but also an accident in which the hit-and-run driver knocks you down while you're standing or walking.

These slight differences give you a clue to what happened. At one time Protective offered coverage only for hit-and-run accidents that happened in New York state. Some years later they added a part that covered "accidents which occur outside of the State of New York but within the United States of America, its territories or possessions, or Canada." While they were at it, they fixed mistakes and omissions in the "hit-and-run" definition, like "after the accident" and "if so." But they also decided to make things a little tougher for the policyholder. Now he has to report the accident to the police within 24 hours or else. And he is given only 30 days instead of 90 to send in his affidavit.

Why didn't they also change the first definition? I have no idea. Sheer sloppiness, I suppose. But the result is that if

I get injured by a hit-and-run driver, I'm a little better off if it happens near my home in New York state than if it happens near my summer home in Nova Scotia, Canada. I'm being punished by Protective for driving my car across the New York state borders.

The trickiness of insurance policy definitions was dramatically illustrated in a 1975 Iowa court case (227 N.W. 2d 169). C & J Fertilizer Inc. was insured against burglary by Allied Mutual. On Sunday, April 18, 1970, C & J's warehouse was broken into and $10,000 worth of chemicals and equipment was stolen. Allied refused to pay. Why? Because the policy defined "burglary" like this:

> "Burglary" means the felonious abstraction of insured property from within the premises by a person making felonious entry therein by actual force and violence, of which force and violence there are visible marks made by tools, explosives, electricity or chemicals upon, or physical damage to, the exterior of the premises at the place of such entry.

There was no physical damage to the outside of the building, Allied said, and so they weren't liable.

The case was first decided by an Iowa trial court, which said Allied didn't have to pay. The policy definition of "burglary" was unambiguous, said the judge. There was nothing in the record "upon which to base a finding that the door to plaintiff's place of business was entered feloniously, by actual force and violence." Case dismissed.

C & J appealed to the Iowa Supreme Court. There certainly had been a burglary, they said, and they could prove it. To begin with, there were tire tracks in the mud outside the building. Second, the chemicals had been stored in a locked room inside the warehouse. The door to that room was damaged and carried visible marks made by tools.

How did the burglar get inside? Answer: He was very good at his job. A witness who was an experienced policeman showed how it was done. He walked up to the overhead plexiglass door of the building, leaned on it hard, turned the locked handle at the same time, and—bingo!—it opened and he was inside. No visible marks outside.

On March 19, 1975, the Supreme Court of Iowa decided the case. Allied had to pay. "The exclusion in issue," the court said, "masking as a definition, makes insurer's obligation to pay turn on the skill of the burglar, not on the event the parties bargained for: a bona fide third party burglary resulting in loss of plaintiff's chemicals and equipment."

As to the policy definition of the word *burglary,* the court said it was "a classic example of that proverbial fine print (six point type) which 'becomes visible only after the event.' Such print is additionally suspect when, instead of appearing logically in the 'exclusions' of the policy, it poses as a part of an esoteric definition of burglary.... The president of C & J, a 37-year-old farmer with a high school education, looked at that portion of the policy setting out coverages, including coverage for burglary loss, the amounts of insurance, and the 'location and description.' He could not recall reading the fine print defining 'burglary' on page 3 of the policy.... The liability-avoiding provision of the definition of 'burglary' is, in the circumstances of this case, unconscionable."

What do all these examples prove? They prove—conclusively, I think—that definitions don't belong in a legal document. If they just echo the dictionary, they are pointless—like section 441(d) of the Internal Revenue Code, which says, "For purposes of this subtitle, the term 'calendar year' means a period of 12 months ending on December 31." If they *don't* echo the dictionary but sneak in something extra, they're a piece of trickery and should always be replaced by a straightforward explanation in the text of the document.

7

How to Find Examples

In October, 1972, Congress passed the Consumer Product Safety Act. It said manufacturers must report at once to the new Consumer Product Safety Commission all products with a defect that "could create a substantial product hazard."

What is a defect? The commission proposed the following definition:

A "defect" within the meaning of section 15 of the CPSA is any aspect of a product which creates an unnecessary risk of injury. Such aspects include, but are not limited to the following: Performance, composition, contents, design, construction, finish, packaging, warnings, and instructions. A product presents an unnecessary risk if the aspect which creates the risk is not necessary for the product to perform its functional purpose. A risk is also unnecessary if the benefits (including recreational and aesthetic benefits) to be gained from use of the product do not justify the risk of injury. A product defect within the meaning of section 15 includes both unintended manufacturing errors and / or imperfections and intended product aspects.

That definition wasn't clear at all. Dozens of companies and consumer groups wrote in to say so. The commission considered all those comments and drafted several other definitions. None of them solved the problem. Finally the commission gave up. It decided to do without a definition but simply offer examples of the kinds of defects that would have to be reported. Their final regulation contained no definition of *defect* but simply listed five examples. Here is a Plain English version of what it said:

What kinds of defects you must report.
    You must report any kind of defect that may cause an unnecessary risk of injury. It may be a defect in production, design, labeling, warnings or instructions.
    Example 1. A microwave oven poses a shock hazard because its casing may be electrically charged by full-line voltage. The defect is due to a production error.
    Example 2. Shoes labeled as good for long-distance running may cause muscle or tendon injury if so used. The defect is due to mislabeling.
    Example 3. A power mower is sold without proper instructions and safety warnings. Misuse by consumers may cause injuries. The defect lies in the lack of proper warnings.
    Example 4. A kite has a thin coating of metal that adds to its beauty. The kite also handles better because of the extra weight. But it carries a risk of electrocu-

tion since it may get entangled in powerlines. The defect is due to faulty design because that possibility has not been considered.

Example 5. A kitchen knife has a sharp blade that can seriously hurt a user. This is not a defect since the sharp blade is needed for proper use of the knife.

This is a good model of how to use examples. What the commission tried to do was to guide companies that must comply with the law. Normally that wouldn't be hard. If a new product comes on the market and there's something wrong with it, consumers are soon heard from. The person who first got a shock from that defective oven surely let the makers know about it. But, when it comes to defects of design, labeling or poor instructions, it's not so easy to draw the line. There may be quite an argument about such subtle defects as the metal coating on the kite.

So whenever anything is complex and hard to explain, use examples. It's the only way to put complicated matters in Plain English. In a legal document that deals with rules, conditions and contingencies, plenty of good examples are an absolute must.

Lawyers always hesitate to use examples. It's the old story—they're scared of Judge Fiendish. If I use examples, the lawyer says to himself, sooner or later a judge will say a situation I *haven't* mentioned was left out on purpose. Examples are dangerous. Let's stay away from them and put them into explanatory regulations, brochures, flyers—anywhere but in the text of a legal document.

Nothing could be more wrong. If a rule is difficult to write, examples must be right there where the reader needs them to understand what is meant. To repeat what I've said before, never mind Judge Fiendish. If you want to pacify him, use the tried-and-true formula "including but not limited to." Or say in Plain English, "The examples given here are for illustration only. There are many other cases."

How many examples should you use? The only answer I can give you is, as many as are needed. Often a single example will do, but to explain a difficult concept, like a defect that may cause injury, you need at least three and maybe five or more. Why do I use these odd figures? Because statistically the possible cases will form a bell-shaped so-called normal curve. Most of the typical cases will be bunched in the middle and the rare situations will form thin fringes. Most manufacturing defects are like the shock-producing oven, and items like the shiny but deadly kite are rare. And you must mention the kitchen knife that's dangerous but need *not* be reported to the commission.

And where do you find examples? Don't—please don't— try to make them up. Instead, look around. Each clause in a legal document must have a purpose. Why are you saying this? Because you want to cover such-and-such. All right, put the thing you're aiming at right in as an example. Add more examples until you have covered the whole range of possibilities. Don't try to think them up—find them right under your nose or in the files. That kite wasn't a figment of somebody's imagination—it existed and endangered a real child.

A few years ago I was hired by an insurance company to simplify one of their policies. I filled it to the brim with examples.

How did I find them? I was not an insurance man, so I asked Cynthia, the underwriter I worked with, to get me copies of actual case files. She was extremely helpful and during a weekend went to a nearby agency to find suitable material. A few days later I got a fat package in the mail. I studied all those cases and picked those that illustrated points that were tough to explain.

The policy was a so-called umbrella policy that covered liabilities beyond what is covered by regular policies. For instance, the usual automobile policy covers liabilities for personal injuries up to $300,000. The umbrella policy covered possible jury verdicts up to a million. This was expressed in the original policy as follows:

> The Company will indemnify the Insured for all sums which the Insured shall be legally obligated to pay as damages and expenses, all as more fully defined by the term "Ultimate Net Loss," on account of:
> 1. personal injuries, including death at any time resulting therefrom;
> 2. property damage.

To explain that basic point, I used the example of an actual case. I'll never forget the shock when I saw the actual settlement of the case for $1,000,000. What I wrote was this:

> If you have an accident covered by your auto insurance, we'll pay the difference between what's payable under that policy and the sum total of what you legally have to pay up to the liability limit shown on the attached declarations page.
>
> *Example.* You miss a stop sign and crash into a motorcycle. Its 28-year-old married driver is paralyzed from the waist down and will spend the rest of his life in a wheelchair. A jury says you have to pay him $1,300,000. Your standard insurance liability limit is $300,000. We'll pay the balance of $1,000,000.

Another clause in the original policy said:

> The Insured shall promptly reimburse the Company for 50% of any amount of ultimate net loss paid on behalf of the Insured but the amount payable by the Insured (here-

inafter referred to as the retained limit) shall not exceed the maximum retained limit stated in Item 4 (a) of the Declarations.

The maximum deductible in all those umbrella policies was $250. I felt I had to explain this point with two examples, one where the damage was under $500 and one where it was more. Again, I adapted one of the actual cases:

If a liability covered by this policy is not covered by another policy of yours or anyone else insured, we'll pay claims you legally have to pay up to the limit listed on the attached declarations page. However, you'll have to pay a small deductible of 50% up to the first $500—in other words, no more than $250.

Example. You've boarded your neighbor's poodle while they're away on vacation. You're careless and the poodle runs away and gets lost. Your neighbors insist on your paying for the loss. If he was an ordinary poodle worth say $400, you pay $200 and we pay $200. But if he was a prize-winning show dog worth $4,000, you pay $250 and we pay $3,750.

A third clause in the original policy said:

With respect to any occurrence not covered by the underlying policy(ies) of insurance described in Schedule A hereof or any other underlying insurance collectible by the Insured but covered by the terms and conditions of this policy except for the amount of retained limit specified below, the Company shall:

(A) defend such suit against the Insured alleging such injury or destruction and seeking damages on account thereof, even if such suit is groundless, false or fraudulent; but the Company may make such investigation, negotiation and settlement of any claim or suit as it deems expedient.

It took me a while to find a case that wasn't covered by the normal auto or homeowners policy, but eventually I found one. With a few adaptations, it served as a neat example. My Plain English policy said:

> In those cases where this policy protects you against claims not covered in any of your other policies, we'll do much more for you than just pay for legal liabilities.
>
> We'll defend any suit for damages against you or anyone else insured even if it's groundless or fraudulent. And we'll investigate, negotiate and settle on your behalf any claim or suit if that seems to us proper and wise.
>
> *Example.* You own a two-family house and rent the second-floor apartment to the Miller family. The Millers don't pay the rent and you finally have to evict them. Out of sheer spite, they sue you for wrongful eviction. You're clearly in the right, but the defense of the suit costs $750. Under this policy we defend you and win the case in court. The whole business doesn't cost you a penny.

I'm still quite proud of that first Plain English insurance policy I wrote, with all those memorable examples. (You need a lost poodle or a vindictive Miller family to bring home a point.) In a recent medical group insurance certificate I rewrote, I used the same system. Again, I collected as many examples as I could from George, the underwriter I worked with.

For instance, one clause in the original certificate read as follows:

> If you have with respect to yourself or your dependents satisfied the Applicable Deductible Amount provision of the group policy three times during any one calendar year, in accordance with all the terms and conditions of

the "Benefit Provision" of the group policy, the Applicable Cash Deductible shall be waived thereafter for the balance of that calendar year only with respect to you and your dependents.

I studied this paragraph for a long time, but simply couldn't figure out what it meant. Finally I asked George. He said it was very simple. There was a $100 deductible per family member per year.

Obviously this had to be explained, with an example of a family of four. I wrote:

Cash deductible maximum.

There is a maximum of three cash deductibles per family per year. Each insured family member has his or her own deductible. If each of three insured family members has paid the deductible in a calendar year, we waive the deductible for any other family member for the rest of the year.

Example. Angelo Vaccaro has a wife and two sons, Vincent and Anthony. He has two claims early in the year, for four office visits to a dermatologist and for five days in the hospital with a broken leg. In August his wife sees her doctor six times because of migraine headaches. In October Vincent is treated for a broken collarbone. In December Anthony comes down with the flu. Vaccaro's plan has a $100 deductible per person. He pays $300 for himself, his wife and Vincent, but nothing for Anthony.

Another section of the certificate dealt with coverage of total disability. Typically, the information was buried in a long definition. It said:

"Total Disability" means, during any one continuous period of disability commencing while you are insured hereunder,

(A) from the onset of such period of disability through

the first twenty-four months for which benefits are paid, your complete inability, due to Injury or Sickness, to perform any and every duty pertaining to your occupation, and

(B) thereafter, if the Schedule of Insurance provides benefits in excess of twenty-four months, your complete inability, due to Injury or Sickness, to engage in any reasonably gainful occupation for which you are or may become fitted by education, training or experience, having due regard for the nature of your occupation at the time you became disabled and for your prior average earnings.

Again, I was completely stumped. What did this mean? George explained. "Well," he said, "you take a salesman who makes a lot of money. We don't want to force him to accept a low-paying job as a janitor or something. Of course, if he decides he *wants* to take the job, that's another story. Then we'd stop our payments."

Armed with this information, I wrote:

Total disability means you're unable to do any duties of your current job. This applies from the start of your disability through the first two years. Then, if your plan pays for more than two years, it means you're unable to work at any job for which you are or may become fitted by education, training or experience. We'll consider the nature of your job when you got disabled and your average earnings at that time. But we won't pay while you do any work for wages or profit.

Example. Philip Grabowski works as a traveling salesman. He earns $50,000 a year. He has a heart attack and his doctor says he must stop traveling. He is offered a $7,000 janitor job he could fill even with his weak heart. But since this is so far below the job he held when he had the heart attack, we pay him his disability income in spite of that offer. If he decides to take the janitor job, we'll stop our payments.

You see what this does? Without a proper example, it would be extremely hard to explain it to a layman.

Let me add a word about names. I called the two people in the examples Vaccaro and Grabowski. I didn't call them A or B or Jones or Brown because I think examples should be as vivid as possible. And where did I find the names Vaccaro and Grabowski? In my local phone book, of course. It has thousands of equally vivid names, all splendidly suitable for examples.

And now, just to show you what *not* to do, here are two examples written by the U.S. Department of Labor. They are from a regulation spelling out what's meant by an "hour of service" in the Pension Reform Act. There are 19 examples. One of them says:

> An employee has a regularly scheduled 5-day, 40-hour week. During a computation period the employee works for the first week, spends the second week on paid vacation, returns to work for an hour and is then disabled for the remainder of the computation period. Payments under a disability plan maintained by the employer are made to the employee on account of the period of disability. The employee is credited with 582 hours of service for the computation period (40 hours for the period of paid vacation; 41 hours for the performance of duties; 501 hours for the period of disability).

This doesn't look like anything that could happen in real life, but let's try to fit a situation to the example. Let's say Amanda Bumstead (to give the poor anonymous employee a phone book name) works steadily for one week early in January. Then she takes a week's vacation, but the weather is lousy. She comes back on the brink of pneumonia but, thinking of those precious hours of service she needs for her pension plan, she drags herself to the office on Monday morning. There she sits at her desk, coughing miserably and arousing sympathy among her fellow employees. Finally, at 10 A.M., they can't stand it any longer and talk her into going home. She's hospitalized and later sent to a convalescent home. She doesn't show up again at the office for over a year. (Later she learns that her heroic hour at the office was pointless, since she needed no more than 501 hours of service.)

Another Department of Labor example says this:

> Employee B has no regular work schedule. As a result of an injury, B is incapacitated for 1 day. A lump-sum payment of $500 is made to B with respect to the injury under an insurance program maintained by the employer. A pension plan maintained by the employer provides for the calculation of the number of hours of service to be credited to an employee without a regular work schedule on the basis of an 8-hour day. B is therefore required to be credited with no more than 8 hours for the day during which he was incapacitated, even though B's rate of pay immediately before the injury was $3.00 per hour.

This is where my imagination fails me. What could possibly have happened to B? (I'll call him Roderick Higgins.) He has a job without regular hours, he's paid $3 for each hour on the job, but he struggles on, happy in the thought that he has accident insurance and a pension plan. Then something happens which keeps him away from work for only one day but costs $500 in doctor bills and medical care. What could it have been? Was he run over by a bus, spending one $500 day in the hospital and going back to work the next day? Or did he use a long weekend to have his appendix taken out?

I'm afraid I'll never know. Maybe if the regulation writer in the Department of Labor reads this, he'll let me know what really happened to poor Roderick.

8

The Cross-Reference Habit

In its regulations under the Pension Reform Act, the U.S. Labor Department explains how to write Plain English plan summaries for employees: "It will usually require the limitation or elimination of technical jargon and of long, complex sentences, the use of clarifying examples and illustrations, the use of clear cross-references and a table of contents."

That's excellent advice, except for the business about cross-references. Nothing could be more pernicious. Cross-references, far from helping readers to understand, poison any attempt to write clearly and simply. The ordinary reader considers cross-references an unmitigated nuisance. His eyes refuse to even see them.

The front page of today's *New York Times* has eight major stories. They all break off with a reference to an inside page—"Continued on Page 41, Column 1," "Continued on

Page 21, Column 2," "Continued on Page 86, Column 3," and so on. How many readers follow up those stories? A handful out of 700,000, I should guess. The rest just let it go, fully convinced that the important parts of each story are on page 1 and whatever is buried on inside pages is not worth bothering with.

In trying to write Plain English, some lawyers have learned to consider the reading level of unsophisticated readers, but they rarely consider their reading *habits.* One of those habits is that they'll ignore all cross-references, footnotes, anything that distracts them from the page and line they're reading. The *Times* may have all kinds of juicy bits in continued stories on page 21 or 86, but for most readers they might as well be blank. Cross-references, for most American adults, are meaningless clutter.

Now consider the document-drafting lawyer. Not only has he fallen into the habit of defining every other word in a separate section, but he always prefers a cross-reference to an explanation on the spot. It's the lazy man's way to write. Why say it again if he's already explained it before? People can look it up, can't they?

Yes they can, but they won't. They will cheerfully let it go by. If their ignoring of cross-references will make a passage wholly meaningless, they don't care. Probably they won't even notice.

In my rewriting of FTC regulations, replacing cross-references soon became an invariable routine. For instance, the original funeral rule said:

Retention of documents.

To assure compliance with the provisions of this part, and prevent future use of the unfair and deceptive practices it prohibits, all funeral homes subject to the provisions of this part shall be required to retain and to make available for inspection by Federal Trade Commission officials, upon request, true and accurate copies of the written disclosures of price lists required by section 453.3(a)(2) and 453.5(b)(1), (d)(1), and (e)(1), and all revisions thereof, for at least three years after the date of their last distribution to customers, and a copy of each selection memorandum signed by a customer, as required by section 453.5(f)(1), for at least three years from the date on which the memorandum was signed.

In Plain English this became:

Recordkeeping.

You must keep exact copies of the following. If Federal Trade Commission staff members ask for them, you must have them ready.

(a) Permissions to embalm. If the permission is not given in writing, you must keep a record of who gave it and when. You must keep copies for at least three years.

(b) Casket, outer burial container and general price lists, together with all revisions. You must keep copies for at least three years from the date you last gave one to a customer.

(c) Funeral agreements. You must keep copies for at least three years from the date of signing.

You see? I replaced each cross-reference with a brief statement of what it referred to. (The permissions to embalm were added after the hearings.)

Again, in the original FTC home insulation rule I found this paragraph:

Liability.
An industry member shall be liable under this Part if he

•   •   •

(3) represents an R-value under section 460.4 or section 460.6 that is not based on the applicable test procedure set forth in section 460.3; *Provided, however,* That an industry member who is not a manufacturer shall be liable under this subsection only if he has actual knowledge fairly implied on the basis of objective circumstances, that the R-value is not based on the applicable test procedures.

In my rewrite I dropped the section references and wrote:

Liability.
Labs are liable if they give industry members R-values or related data not proved by the proper test methods. Industry members are liable if they show in labels, fact sheets, ads, or elsewhere R-values that are not based on tests done with the proper methods. However, if your company is not a lab, you are liable only if you know or should know that those test methods were not used or that the R-values or related data are wrong.

Replacing the section numbers with simple explanations made the section much more intelligible. Remember that this section fixes a liability that may cost a company $10,000 a day in penalties. And, by the way, look at how I translated "knowledge fairly implied on the basis of objective circumstances" into "you should know." I suggested that simple wording to my friends, the FTC lawyers, and they went along without a murmur. Even when scrutinized by Judge Fiendish, the translation means exactly the same as the original. If an installer of home insulation uses some plastic foam and it's clearly thinner than other stuff marked with the same R-value (heat resistance), he's liable. In Plain English, "he should know."

Let's go on to a third example. The original FTC hearing aid rule said:

> No seller shall represent that any hearing aid can eliminate unwanted noise; *Provided, however,* That it shall not be a violation of section 440.9(m) to represent accurately the ability of a hearing aid with a telephone option to attenuate acoustical background signals, if such is the fact.

When I read this the first time, I naturally looked through the whole lengthy regulation to find section 440.9(m). To my surprise I found that this was a boomerang reference to the section itself. The writer was so steeped in the cross-reference habit that he referred to the paragraph he was writing by its section number. (Doubtless he always referred to himself as "the undersigned.")

Anyway, there was no cross-reference—or boomerang reference—in my Plain English version. It said:

Background noise.
Do not say or imply that any hearing aid can shut out all unwanted background noise. You can explain that a hearing aid with a phone option can reduce background noise while the wearer is using the phone, but only if this is true.

From "attenuate acoustical background signals" to "reduce background noise." Not bad, is it?

However, these scattered cross-references in reasonably short FTC rules are easily taken care of. It's more of a problem if you're dealing with a longer document drafted by confirmed cross-reference addicts. That encyclopedia of gobbledygook, the Internal Revenue Code, teems with them. There's hardly a sentence that doesn't send the reader to another place in the 1,600-page volume. And, since that other place, as likely as not, is also filled to the brim with cross-references, the whole monstrous mass of prose has become a seamless web, a tropical jungle of crisscross connections, taking specialists years to disentangle.

For the Treasury and Ways and Means Committee lawyers, who are the culprits of this monumental obfuscation, simple references from one section to another are no longer interesting. Since they have to have their daily dose of cross-references, they've long ago learned to deal with the problem of the cross-reference that doesn't fit. You want to refer the reader from section 1139 to section 1705 even though section 1705 doesn't contain the exact answer? Easy. You give the reader a qualified or "as if" reference.

Take for example section 1442(a) of the Internal Revenue Code. It fixes rules for withholding taxes on foreign corporations. The rules are a little like the rules for withholding taxes on nonresident aliens in section 1441 and there's also a faint resemblance to the rules for withholding taxes on tax-free bonds in section 1451. For the cross-reference artist this is a lovely opportunity to assemble a rich bouquet:

> In the case of foreign corporations subject to taxation under this subtitle, there shall be deducted and withheld at the source in the same manner and on the same items of income as is provided in section 1441 or section 1451 a tax equal to 30 percent thereof; except that, in the case of interest described in section 1451 (relating to tax-free covenant bonds), the deduction and withholding shall be at the rate specified therein. For purposes of the preced-

ing sentence, the references in section 1441(b) to sections 871(a)(1)(C) and (D) shall be treated as referring to sections 881(a)(3) and (4), the reference in section 441(c)(1) to section 871(b)(2) shall be treated as referring to section 842 or section 882(a)(2), as the case may be, the reference in section 1441(c)(5) to section 871(a)(1)(D) shall be treated as referring to section 881(a)(4), and the reference in section 441(c)(8) to section 871(a)(1)(C) shall be treated as referring to section 881(a)(3).

Or have a look at section 503(b)(3). It deals with foreign tax credits for certain public utilities. Of course there's a definition of public utilities in the Code, but it doesn't quite fit the situation. So the Code writers used one of their "as if" cross-references:

For purposes of paragraph (2), a corporation is a regulated public utility only if it is a regulated public utility within the meaning of subparagraph (A) (other than clauses (ii) and (iii) thereof) or (D) of section 7701(a)(33). For purposes of the preceding sentence, the limitation contained in the last two sentences of section 7701(a)(33) shall be applied as if subparagraphs (A) through (F) inclusive, of section 7701(a)(33) were limited to subparagraphs (A)(i) and (D) thereof.

You'll never believe what this little nest of cross-references means. It simply means that foreign tax credits for utilities don't apply to public transportation.

Some connoisseurs of Revenue writing consider the following the finest "as if" reference of them all. It's the last sentence of section 509(a).

For purposes of paragraph (3), an organization described in paragraph (2) shall be deemed to include an organization described in section 501(c)(4), (5), or (6)

> which would be described in paragraph (2) if it were an
> organization described in section 501(c)(3).

And now let me give you a brief rundown of the treatment of the American family in the Internal Revenue Code. This will take a while, but it's highly instructive.

In the beginning there was the problem of the stockholder who bought stock in the name of another family member to avoid taxes. To plug this little loophole was easy. Section 318(a)(1)(A) says:

> An individual shall be considered as owning the stock
> owned, directly or indirectly, by or for—
> (i) his spouse (other than a spouse who is legally separated from the individual under a decree of divorce or separate maintenance), and
> (ii) his children, grandchildren, and parents.

But people kept on buying stock in the names of family members. After they'd caught on to section 318(a)(1)(A), they started using the names of brothers and sisters. So the next time the Revenue Code writers got around to family stock ownership they spread the net a little wider. This is section 267(c)(4):

> The family of an individual shall include only his brothers and sisters (whether by the whole or half blood), spouse, ancestors, and lineal descendants.

Obviously the government tax lawyers tried to solve the problem once and for all. Let's include step-brothers and step-sisters, they said, and while we're at it, great-grandparents and great-grandchildren. Let's make it "ancestors" instead of "parents" and "descendants" instead of "children and grandchildren." And let's say "lineal" rather than "collateral" descendants because there's not enough evidence of taxpayers buying or selling stock in the names of their nephews or nieces.

Time passes, and the Revenue lawyers have to do something about family ownership of restricted stock options. They use the pattern of section 267(c)(4) and write section 425(d)(1):

> The individual with respect to whom such limitation is being determined shall be considered as owning the stock, directly or indirectly, by and for his brothers and sisters (whether by the whole or half blood), spouse, ancestors, and lineal descendants.

The Internal Revenue Code gets changed every few years but the problem of the taxpayer's family deals doesn't go away. In due course the Revenue lawyers are up against "prohibited transactions" with tax-exempt nonprofit organizations. By now they are slaves of the cross-reference habit. In section 503(b) they write:

> The term "prohibited transaction" means any transaction in which an organization subject to the provisions of this section engages in any transaction which results in a substantial diversion of its income or corpus to a member of the family (as defined in section 267(c)(4)) of an individual who is the creator of such trust or who has made a substantial contribution to such organization.

After that, the Revenue lawyers really get into their stride. Wherever they look, they find taxpayers making family deals. For instance, they have to fix rules for family ownership of personal holding companies. In section 544 (a)(2) they write:

> An individual shall be considered as owning the stock owned, directly or indirectly, by or for his family. For purposes of this paragraph, the family of an individual includes only his brothers and sisters (whether by the whole or half blood), spouse, ancestors, and lineal descendants.

As you see, the Revenue lawyers have taken a big step forward. Instead of being lazy and simply referring to section 267(c)(4), they've copied it verbatim and left out the cross-reference. They've thrown away their beloved crutch.

But not for long. A few years later, small businesses get an extra first-year depreciation allowance. What happens if they've bought the new equipment from a relative? Then they lose the extra depreciation. Section 179(a)(2) says:

> For purposes of paragraph (1), the term "purchase" means any acquisition of property, but only if—
>
> (A) the property is not acquired from a person whose relationship to the person acquiring it would result in the disallowance of losses under section 267 (but, in applying section 267(b) and (c) for purposes of this section, paragraph (4) of section 267(c) shall be treated as providing that the family of an individual shall include only his spouse, ancestors, and lineal descendants).

We're back again with the cross-reference crutch. But an interesting thing has happened. Taxpayers are no longer likely to make tax-saving arrangements with their brothers and sisters. Family ties have loosened since the first cross-reference to section 267(c)(4), and brothers and sisters have to be subtracted.

The years go by and Revenue lawyers use their new reduced formula in various places. Section 178(b)(2) deals with leases within a family, section 44(c)(3) with buying a new home from a family member, section 1235 with buying a family member's patent. In all these matters the Revenue Code refers to good old section 267(c)(4), always carefully subtracting brothers and sisters.

Then, in 1970, Congress decides to plug the private foundation loophole. In financial deals with a private foundation, the founder's family members are "disqualified persons." Section 4946(d) spells out who they are:

> For purposes of subsection (a)(1), the family of any in-
> dividual shall include only his spouse, ancestors, lineal
> descendants, and spouses of lineal descendants.

Once again, the Revenue lawyers have thrown away the
cross-reference crutch. Why? Well, by now they've taken
the family circle of section 267(c)(4), subtracted the brothers and sisters and *added* a new class of relatives, sons-in-
law and daughters-in-law. It seems that after the brothers
and sisters drifted away, wealthy taxpayers have begun to
use their sons-in-law and daughters-in-law for their tax-
avoiding schemes.

After that 1970 breakaway, the Revenue lawyers
yearned for their old cross-reference crutch. Sure, the reference to section 267(c)(4) was no longer very useful, since
one class of relatives had to be subtracted and another one
added. But that shouldn't make a cross-reference impossible. When the 1974 Pension Reform Act came along, the
cross-reference to section 267(c)(4) was reinstalled, minus
brothers and sisters but plus sons-in-law and daughters-in-
law. The feat was accomplished in sections 4975(e)(5) and
(6):

> (5) The ownership and profits and beneficial interests
> shall be determined in accordance with the rules for con-
> structive ownership of stock provided in section 267(c)
> (other than paragraph (3) thereof), except that section
> 267(c)(4) shall be treated as providing that the members
> of the family of an individual are the members within the
> meaning of paragraph (6).
> (6) The family of any individual shall include his
> spouse, ancestors, lineal descendants, and any spouse
> of a lineal descendant.

Two years pass. Now it's 1976 and a new amendment to
the Revenue Code limits the campaign expenses of a presi-

dential candidate and his immediate family. Who belongs to the immediate family? Section 9035(b) explains:

> The term "immediate family" means a candidate's spouse, and any child, parent, grandparent, brother, half-brother, sister, or half-sister of the candidate, and the spouses of such persons.

Different again. Grandchildren are out, but brothers-in-law and sisters-in-law are in.

That same year 1976 gives Revenue lawyers an opportunity to describe a *really* large family. Oddly enough, it's an amendment that has to do with accounting methods. Corporations must use the accrual method, but farming corporations can continue the old-fashioned cash method *if* most of the stock belongs to members of the same family. Section 447(d)(1) explains who they are:

> The members of the same family are an individual, such individual's brothers and sisters, the brothers and sisters of such individual's parents and grandparents, the ancestors and lineal descendants of any of the foregoing, a spouse of any of the foregoing, and the estate of any of the foregoing.

Can you see in your mind's eye the picture of the cash-accounting farm family? There they are, thirty, forty, fifty of them—sitting for an old-fashioned family portrait. The oldest brother and his wife sit in the middle, with uncles, aunts and cousins, a toothless great-uncle and a bent grandmother, a few babies here and there, in-laws, cousins and a stray second cousin once removed. Even though they're now stockholders in a corporation, they still have the blessing of the federal government if they stick to the old way of cash accounting, just like great-grandpa, who started the family farm back in the last century.

Is this the end of the family saga of the Internal Revenue

Code? Not quite. It's two years later now and the Revenue Act of 1978 adds a new wrinkle to the cash-accounting corporate family farm. They're now allowed to give stock to employees and to members of *their* families. And who are those family members? Section 447(h)(1)(B)(ii)(I) tells us. They're family members "within the meaning of section 267(c)(4)."

The Revenue lawyers have come full circle. They started with a simple cross-reference to section 267(c)(4), subtracted from it, added to it, left it out, reinstated it, abandoned it for the glamour of presidential candidates' families and the nostalgia of the old-time family farm, and finally came back to it. Someday, maybe, those family farm employees will want to give stock in the farm to their sons-in-law and daughters-in-law and the cross reference will have to be changed again.

But that's for the future. Or could it possibly be that someday in the future the Internal Revenue Code will be rewritten in Plain English? Without a single cross-reference?

I can dream, can't I?

9

Double Negativism

Most lawyers suffer from double negativism. This doesn't mean they're using bad grammar. I have yet to see a legal document that says something like "Don't do nothing illegal." But I've seen thousands with phrases like "A trust shall not constitute a qualified trust unless ... " That's good grammar but an obstacle to easy reading.

In colloquial idiomatic English, double negatives reinforce each other, as in "I shouldn't wonder if it didn't rain," "We couldn't scarcely see a thing" or "She never goes hardly nowhere." The double negatives *don't* cancel each other out.

But in lawyers' English they do. Legal documents teem with negative words like *not, unless, fail to, notwithstanding, except, other than, unlawful, disallowed, refusal, terminate, exempt, void, nonrecognition, denial, insufficient* and thousands more. Each time two negative words are used in the same sentence, the reader has to do a mental switch from no to yes. This goes against the idiomatic grain and makes reading hard.

In translating FTC regulations into Plain English, I kept turning double negatives into positives. Each time I read a phrase like "not unless" I changed it to "only if." Each time I read "it is unlawful to fail to," I changed it to "you must." Gradually this became second nature to me. For the rest of this chapter I'll give you examples of this technique. I hope it will become second nature to you too.

Let's start with a few examples from my FTC experience. For instance, the original FTC home insulation rule said:

> *No* advertisement shall state that the advertised insulation is or may be eligible for tax credits or deductions
> (1) *until* the tax credit or deduction has become law, and
> (2) *unless* the advertised insulation meets any eligibility requirements which may be imposed.

You see how double negativism works? "*No* advertisement shall . . . *until* . . . and *unless.*" The trick is to turn the second negative into a positive. Like this:

> Do not claim any tax benefit for your products in ads, labels or elsewhere. *You can do this only when* a tax benefit has become law and your product qualifies for it.

Let's take another example. This is from an FTC warranty rule:

> It is a violation of the Federal Trade Commission Act for a warrantor offering a full warranty to require as a condition of securing a remedy, any *unreasonable* duty. The following are unreasonable duties:

•   •   •

(h) Requiring that a consumer give notice of a defect within a specified period of time *other than* a "reasonable period of time."

Pure double negativism. "It is a violation to require any *unreasonable* duty. . . . Requiring notice within a period *other than.*" Let's switch the second negative to a positive:

You must not say in a full warranty that customers have to tell you about a defect within a certain time. But *you can ask them* to tell you within "a reasonable time."

My third FTC example comes from the original version of the funeral rule:

It is an *unfair* or deceptive act or practice for any funeral service industry member *to fail to* provide by telephone, upon consumer request, accurate information regarding the funeral service industry member's retail prices of funeral products and services.

Let's change the double negative into a positive—and throw out all those needless words while we're at it.

If anyone asks by phone about your charges for goods and services, *you must quote* your exact prices.

Of course, double negativism is not confined to the FTC. It flourishes wherever laws, regulations and legal documents are written. Here's a neat example from the 1978 Petroleum Marketing Practices Act. It aims to protect gas station franchise holders. Section 102(a)(2) says:

The following are grounds of termination or nonrenewal:

•   •   •

(D) An agreement in writing between the franchisor and the franchisee to terminate or not to renew if—

• • •

(iii) within 7 days after the date on which the franchisee is provided a copy of such agreement, the franchisee has *not* posted by certified mail a written notice to the franchisor *repudiating* such agreement.

What have we here? A list of four grounds for stopping the franchise (A, B, C, D), the last of which is simply a mutual agreement. So far so good. But at the tail end of (D), after two lengthy clauses, (i) and (ii), there's suddenly a double negative that says the cancellation agreement is no good if the franchise holder writes back to say he's changed his mind. I read this several times and didn't catch on to what clause (iii) meant. The only way to make it clear is to turn the two negatives into a positive. Like this:

You can stop or not renew a franchise by mutual agreement. If so, you must send the franchise holder a copy of that agreement. *He then has seven days* from the day he got the copy *to say he has changed his mind and wants to stay on.* He must put this in a letter and send it to you by certified mail.

Next example. Let's look at the federal Warranty Act and its definition of "remedy."

The term "remedy" means whichever of the following sections the warrantor elects:
    (A) repair,
    (B) replacement, or
    (C) refund;
except that the warrantor may *not* elect refund *unless*
        (i) the warrantor is *unable* to provide replacement and repair is *not* commercially practicable or *cannot* be timely made, or
        (ii) the consumer is willing to accept such refund.

This is one of those definitions that make legal documents an obstacle course. The drafters of the Warranty Act, searching for a word that would include repair, replacement and refund, hit upon the ill-fitting word *remedy.* Once they'd done that, they had to define it. And once they'd done *that,* they yielded to the temptation to include the rule about refunds in the definition of *remedy.*

The result is one of the finest examples of a *triple* negative in legal writing. "The warrantor may *not . . . unless . . .* the warrantor is *unable."* Let's turn it into a set of positives:

> To make good on your warranty, *you must repair or replace* the defective part or product. *You can refund the money only if* you cannot replace the part or product and repairs would cost too much money or take too much time.
>
> Otherwise *you can refund the money only if* the customer agrees.

From a triple negative, let's go on to a quadruple negative. You don't believe there is such a thing? Never underestimate the Internal Revenue lawyers. Section 401(a)(11) of the Internal Revenue Code deals with pension plans. It says:

> A trust shall *not* constitute a qualified trust if the plan provides for an annuity *unless* such plan provides for a qualified joint and survivor annuity.
>
> •   •   •
>
> (D) A plan shall *not* be treated as *not* satisfying the requirements of this paragraph solely because the spouse of the participant is *not* entitled to receive a survivor annuity *unless* the participant and his spouse have been married throughout the 1-year period ending on the date of such participant's death.

Yes, it's a true quadruple negative. "A plan shall *not* be
... *not* satisfying ... solely because the spouse is *not* entitled ... *unless.*"

How do you solve a baffling problem like this? It isn't
easy. You have to remind yourself over and over again that
two minuses make a plus, three minuses make a plus and a
minus, and four minuses make two pluses. "A plan shall
not be *not* satisfying" means "a plan will satisfy." "A
spouse is *not* entitled *unless*" means "a spouse is entitled
only if."

Let's translate:

> If your plan offers the choice of an annuity, *it must
> also* offer the choice of a joint or survivor annuity for
> husband and wife. But *you can put in* the following
> condition to prevent abuses. *You can say* that when a
> plan member dies, the widow or widower *will get* the
> survivor annuity *only if* the couple has been married
> for at least a year.

Finally, there's the quintuple negative—the ultimate
weapon of the legal writer.

I found only one example of this incredible piece of syn-
tax. It comes from the proposed FTC regulation on credit
practices. Section 444.2(a)(4) says:

> It is an *unfair* act or practice for a lender or a retail in-
> stallment seller directly or indirectly:
>
> (a) to take or receive from a consumer an obligation
> which:
>
> •   •   •
>
> (4) constitutes or contains a security interest *other
> than* a purchase money security interest, *except,* where
> the proceeds of a personal loan are *not* to be primarily
> applied to the purchase of consumer goods, the lender

may take a security interest in *other than* household goods.

What does this mean? When I first read it, I didn't understand a word of it. I reread it several times but simply couldn't figure it out. Later I was told by an FTC lawyer that it was designed to rule out blanket security.

I asked what "blanket security" meant. I then learned about the great American custom of letting a borrower use everything he owns as collateral. Most banks, finance companies and credit unions write into their standard loan agreements that all the borrower's household goods and personal effects will serve as collateral for the loan.

During the hearings on the credit practices rule, witnesses explained that most low-income borrowers have no good collateral to offer. They have no stocks, no bonds, no valuables of any kind. If they have a car, it's not fully paid for. If they have a house, it's mortgaged. The only thing they have is their job.

So the creditor takes their family belongings as collateral. Will he get his money back if they can't keep up the loan payments? Of course not. Those few sticks of furniture are hardly worth picking up and storing. In one case in Illinois, a finance company repossessed a chest of drawers, two end tables, a chair, a bed and a car. They were sold for $81. The outstanding debt was $500.

Then why do creditors insist on blanket security? Because of its psychological effect. A person who is in danger of losing his household furniture and his clothes will do anything to pay his debt. "The real purpose of the practice," one witness said, "is simply to obtain a device to terrorize consumers or to harass them until payments are made on the loans."

Section 444.2(a)(4) was designed to stop this practice.

But whoever wrote it botched the job. There was unanimous agreement at the hearings that the quintuple negative was obscure, ambiguous and in many ways unintelligible. Could stocks or jewelry be used as collateral for a car loan? Could tools of the trade be used as collateral for dancing lessons? Could passbook loans be used to buy home appliances? Could any collateral be used for consolidation loans? Nobody knew what was meant.

After the hearings were over, the presiding officer filed his report. About the quintuple negative he wrote: "This provision of the proposed rule is both illogical and unnecessarily difficult to interpret. . . . If it is intended to prohibit the granting of security interests in household goods or, for that matter, in other property of the sort that would be generally considered essential for the preservation of a reasonable lifestyle, e.g. furniture, clothing, cookware, crockery, tools of the trade, or an automobile necessary to go to and from work, the section should be drafted in such a fashion as to do so."

This is practically a recipe for a Plain English version:

Do not take any of the following as collateral:

(1) Household goods such as furniture, clothes, linen, china, cookware, appliances, TV sets and jewelry.

(2) Tools of the borrower's trade.

(3) A car needed to go to and from work.

However, you can take any of these as collateral for the credit contract or purchase money loan they are bought with.

10

Shredded English

In 1955 a man named Smith was tried in a California court. He had solicited a customer for a prostitute and was accused of the crime of pimping. The law said:

> Any male person who, knowing a female person is a prostitute, lives or derives support or maintenance in whole or in part from the earnings or proceeds of her prostitution, or from money loaned or advanced to or charged against her by any keeper or manager or inmate of a house or other place where prostitution is practiced or allowed, *or who solicits or receives compensation for soliciting for her* is guilty of pimping, a felony.

Smith had a smart lawyer who told the court that Smith was innocent. The law was ambiguous, he said. It could be read to mean "who solicits for her or receives compensation for soliciting for her." Under that interpretation Smith was guilty—he had been caught in the act. But the law could also be read to mean "who solicits compensation or receives compensation." Under that interpretation Smith was innocent. Did he solicit compensation or receive compensation? There was not a shred of evidence that he did. So, since the law could be read in two ways, he should get the benefit of the doubt and be acquitted.

The judge, who must have had a sense of humor, agreed with Smith's lawyer and let him go. It's all in *People v. Smith,* 279 p. 2d 33 (1955).

The case gained a certain amount of fame because it was written up in a legal journal by Professor Layman E. Allen, now at the University of Michigan Law School. Professor Allen felt that laws and other legal documents were teeming with that kind of ambiguity and that this ought to be stopped. He proposed a new system of legal writing based on symbolic logic. Each sentence was to be broken into pieces connected by *and* or *or* and put into a framework of IF and THEN. He called this method "systematic pulverization"—or "normalization"—and said it was the only way to make legal documents fully clear.

A few years later Professor Reed Dickerson of Indiana University wrote his book *The Fundamentals of Legal Drafting.* He was enthusiastic about Professor Allen's "systematic pulverization" method and adapted it for his book. He called it "tabulation" and recommended it strongly to all legal writers.

That was in 1965. Since then the Dickerson type of tabulation has caught on in a big way. Today you can hardly find a law, regulation or other legal document that isn't broken up into (*a*), (*b*), (*c*), (*1*), (*2*), (*3*), (*A*), (*B*), (*C*), (*i*), (*ii*), (*iii*) and so on. The idea seems to be that if it isn't tabulated it isn't legal.

Professor Dickerson says that tabulation helps legal writers because it prevents mistakes in logic. That may be so, but for ordinary readers tabulation is usually a source of utter confusion.

Let me explain why. Let's take Professor Dickerson's prize example of tabulation, section 1201 of the armed forces regulations issued in 1958. It says:

> Upon a determination by the Secretary concerned that a member of a regular component of the armed forces entitled to basic pay, or any other member of the armed forces entitled to basic pay who has been called or ordered to active duty (other than for training) for a period of more than 30 days, is unfit to perform the duties of his office, grade, rank, or rating because of physical disability incurred while entitled to basic pay, the Secretary may retire the member, with retired pay computed under section 1401 of this title, if the Secretary also determines that—
>
> (1) based upon accepted medical principles, the disability is of a permanent nature;
>
> (2) the disability is not the result of the member's intentional misconduct or willful neglect, and was not incurred during a period of unauthorized absence; and
>
> (3) either—
>
> > (A) the member has at least 20 years of service computed under section 1208 of this title; or
> >
> > (B) the disability is at least 30 percent under the standard schedule of rating disabilities in use by the Veterans' Administration at the time of the determination; and either—
> >
> > > (i) the member has at least eight years of service computed under section 1208 of this title;
> > >
> > > (ii) the disability is the proximate result of performing active duty; or
> > >
> > > (iii) the disability was incurred in line of duty in time of war or national emergency.

This piece of tabulation—I call it Shredded English—is simply impossible to understand by reading it once. You have to go over it again and again, maybe even taking notes to sort out all those conditions and exceptions. Even then it's more than likely you'll misunderstand what's being said. The whole system of dividing and subdividing is extremely forbidding. I think it's fair to say that the vast majority of Americans would give up after several tries and ask an expert for help.

Before I go into all the things that are wrong with this indigestible chunk of prose, let me translate it into Plain English:

This section applies to you if you are a member of the armed forces entitled to basic pay. You must be a member of a regular branch or called to active duty— not just training—for more than 30 days.

If you suffer a physical disability that makes you unfit to do your job, you can retire with retired pay, figured under section 1401. But you must first get the Secretary's approval.

You must meet both of these conditions:

(1) Your disability must be permanent. The doctor who says so must follow accepted medical principles.

(2) You must have at least 20 years of service figured under section 1208. If your disability is rated at least 30%, you need only 8 years. It must be rated under the standard VA schedule in use when it started.

If your disability is rated at least 30%, you can also retire with pay even though you served less than 8 years. There are two conditions: either the disability was the direct result of your being on active duty or it happened in line of duty during a war or national emergency.

You can *not* retire with pay if your disability was the result of planned misconduct or willful neglect or if it started while you were AWOL.

On my scale of readability this version rates 62 (Plain English), while the original rates minus 169 (wholly unreadable). Here are some of the reasons why.

First of all, the original is one 225-word sentence. In Shredded English these monstrosities are common. Once you try to fit all conditions, exceptions and alternatives into one logical unit, you invariably wind up with a lot of words, glued together with semicolons and long dashes, but with only one lonely period at the end. That's not normal writing; that's a special, highly sophisticated technique of putting words together so they'll fit a prefabricated logical mold.

But let's not even talk about the enormous length of those shredded sentences. Let's talk about all those "and's" and "or's." Professor Dickerson is downright ecstatic about them. He says, right after quoting the 225-word sentence, "The beauty of the tabular form of presentation is not only that it removes syntactic ambiguity but that it clarifies the structure of a complicated paragraph by exposing to view the 'and's' and 'or's' that tell the reader which provisions are alternative and which are cumulative."

I'm afraid Professor Dickerson got carried away. Shredded English does *not* expose the "and's" and "or's" to view. Instead, it tucks them away at the ends of lines, where the reader is most likely to overlook them. Nothing is more important in this kind of writing than to show clearly the difference between situations that offer a choice and those that call for fulfillment of *all* conditions. You can't possibly do this with inconspicuous little "and's" and "or's"—even if those "and's" and "or's" are put in italics, boldface or capitals. It's just too much for a normal reader to cope with.

The thing to do with conditions and alternatives is to spell them out carefully so they can't be misunderstood. Preface them each time with a sentence like "You must meet *all four* of the following conditions" or "You can do *any one* of these three things." Tell the reader clearly how many items there are and whether they must be added up or not. After that, there's nothing wrong with a list of those items as long as you don't go beyond, say, five. If there are more than five, make two or three lists. And be sure to make each item a separate unit, beginning with a capital letter and ending with a period.

But that's only part of why Shredded English is so confusing. The main reason is that it groups ideas by the rules of symbolic logic rather than by their importance or frequency.

In Shredded English the soldiers and sailors applying for disability retirement are neatly divided into (1) those with a valid doctor's certificate and (2) those whose disability is their own fault. This doesn't make sense. Presumably those who brought their injuries on themselves are only a small minority. Why put them on the same level with all the others? The only sensible thing is to first write about normal cases of disability and then, way down at the bottom, add a word about those who don't qualify.

That's the real reason why Shredded English is so obscure and artificial-sounding. It treats things of the real world as if they were happening in a never-never land of abstract logic. In abstract logic, I suppose, those wounded in battle and those injured while drunk and disorderly can be seen simply as two groups of applicants. The rule and the exception are on the same level. The great majority and the odd case get equal attention under the labels (*1*) and (*2*). Life isn't like that.

I'll illustrate the point with two examples I found in the Internal Revenue Code.

Section 4072(b) says:

> For purposes of this chapter, the term "tread rubber" means any material—
>
> (1) which is commonly or commercially known as tread rubber or camelback; or
>
> (2) which is a substitute for material described in paragraph (1) and is of a type used in recapping or retreading tires.

As you see, this is one of those definitions dear to the heart of the legal writer. Why did he feel he had to define tread rubber? Because there's a tax on it, of course. The preceding section says it's 5¢ a pound. The whole point of giving a definition of tread rubber is to say that the tax also applies to tread rubber substitutes. And so we get a definition that includes genuine and fake tread rubber, neatly presented under the headings (*1*) and (*2*).

Let's stop this nonsense and say it in Plain English:

> The tax on tread rubber also applies to substitutes used for recaps and retreads.

My next example deals with bows and arrows. (The Internal Revenue Code covers everything under the sun, including bows and arrows.) Section 4161(b) says:

> There is hereby imposed upon the sale by the manufacturer, producer or importer—
>
> (A) of any bow which has a draw weight of 10 pounds or more, and

(B) of any arrow which measures 18 inches overall or more in length,
a tax equivalent to 11 percent of the price for which so sold.

What happened here is clear. The legal writer saw the *and* between *bows* and *arrows* and simply couldn't resist. He had to write this section in the approved Shredded English style, dividing it into (A) bows and (B) arrows.

In the process he managed to hide one fact taxpayers will want to know—that bows and arrows below certain minimum measurements are tax-free.

Let's say so in Plain English:

If you make or import bows and arrows, you must pay a tax on each sale. The tax is 11% of your sales price, but bows under 10 pounds draw weight and arrows under 18 inches long are tax-free.

Recently, Shredded English has gone even further. The 1978 revision of the Internal Revenue Code contains section 172(i)(2), which says:

The term "product liability" means—
(A) liability of the taxpayer for damages on account of physical injury or emotional harm to individuals, or damage to or loss of the use of property, on account of any defect in any product which is manufactured, leased, or sold by the taxpayer, but only if
(B) such injury, harm, or damage arises after the taxpayer has completed or terminated operations with respect to, and has relinquished possession of, such product.

Here we have Shredded English in full flower. There's no *and* and no *or*. There's no set of conditions, exceptions or alternatives. There's only one *if* in this sentence, but even that triggered the Shredded English reaction. "Product liability means (A) but only if (B)." *Anything* can be shredded. Where there's a will there's a way.

Let's make it less shiny, plastic and homogenized. Let's simply say in Plain English:

> Product liability is your liability for damages caused by defects of your products. It applies to what you make, lease or sell. It covers physical or emotional harm to people, damage to property and loss of its use. It does *not* cover products still in your possession.

So one basic rule for writing Plain English is, Stay away from Shredded English. You'd think this is obvious, considering the odd, artificial look of Shredded English on a page. But the influence of the Shredded English fans has been so strong that they've made inroads into the Plain English movement. Quite a few of the recent rewriters of legal documents labor under the delusion that Shredded English is easy to read.

For instance, in July, 1977, the Federal Communications Commission published with great fanfare a new regulation on CB radios. It was supposed to be the first Plain English federal regulation. Unfortunately the authors didn't know much about simplification. For one thing, they made each section heading a question, coming up with such absurdities as "How are the key words in these rules defined?" and "How does a non-individual applicant request temporary privileges?"

But, what's much worse, they fell for Shredded English in a number of places. For instance, one section said:

> You are eligible for a CB license if—
> (1) You are an individual eighteen years of age or

older, an association, a partnership, a corporation or a state, territorial, or local governmental unit; and

(2) You are not a foreign government or a representative of a foreign government.

How does that strike you? Plain English? How about "eligible," "individual," "eighteen years of age," "local governmental unit"? Pure bureaucratese, if you ask me.

On my readability scale this piece of so-called simplified English rates a dismal plus 4—only slightly better than the Internal Revenue Code. (The capital initials after (1) and (2) don't change the fact that it's all one sentence.)

Here's a translation into *real* Plain English:

You have to be at least 18 to get a license. Partnerships can get one only if each partner is at least 18.

Corporations and associations can get them too. So can state and local governments. But we don't give them to foreign governments or their agents.

Another victim of the Shredded English hoax is the National Institute of Education, which is part of the Department of Health, Education and Welfare. In July 1978 their Basic Skills Group came out with suggestions for simplifying the federal income tax forms. They proposed several pieces of Shredded English for the instructions to Form 1040. Mind you, in their so-called simplification, they used Shredded English where the Internal Revenue Service had *not* used it. For instance, in the Internal Revenue explanation of the Credit for the Elderly one paragraph said:

No credit is allowed to a nonresident alien unless the nonresident alien and his or her spouse who is a citizen or resident of the United States elect to be taxed on their worldwide income and file a joint return.

The educators changed this to:

> **Nonresident aliens may receive the credit** *only if—*
> **they are married to a resident or citizen of the U.S.;** *and*
> **—they file a joint return;** *and*
> **—they include all worldwide income on that joint return.**

When I tried to put this in Plain English, I found that the rule I gave you in Chapter 9 about turning "not unless" into "only if" didn't apply here. Clearly this was a rare case that shouldn't be put into positive terms. It's better to say:

> You can't get the credit if you're not a U.S. citizen and live abroad. There's only one exception. You can get it if you're married to a U.S. citizen or someone who lives in the U.S. Then both of you must file a joint return and list all your income from anywhere.

After I'd written this, I started thinking. What would be an actual situation where this exception would apply?

Normally a foreigner living abroad doesn't pay U.S. income tax. But if he has money coming from the United States, there's a withholding tax on it.

The Credit for the Elderly is mainly for people over 65 who don't have social security. Now, since almost everybody who has ever worked for an American firm has social security, our elderly foreigner must be someone who gets no pension from an American company. His American income can only be investment income.

Let's say it's his wife who is a U.S. citizen. (It's unlikely that they'll file a joint return while she lives here and he lives abroad.) Let's say she's a housewife who never had a job.

So we have a couple over 65, living abroad. To be entitled to the full $562.50 credit, their combined income must be under $10,000. They can't have any "worldwide" income to speak of, because they wouldn't voluntarily pay U.S. income tax on it if it amounted to anything much. (The Revenue word "worldwide" makes them sound like a multinational corporation.)

Putting all this together, I "constructed" a couple to whom the exception would apply. The husband is 87. He's an émigré from Czarist Russia, Prince Boris Mihailovich Kalergin. He's never done any work in his life since his early days as a cavalry officer. In the 1920s he married an American heiress, Pamela Morganfeller. She's now 79. They live in London, in a small flat in Kensington. The money has long since dwindled to a small parcel of shares in the family company, leaving them in genteel poverty. So, reluctantly, they apply for the $562.50 tax credit.

Fanciful? Maybe. If you can think of a better solution to the puzzle, please let me know.

11

Dear Consumer

Dear Consumer:

Here we are at the last chapter of my book. You've learned that any kind of legalese can be translated into Plain English. You've also learned that the superiority of "clear, unambiguous" legal language is sheer myth and that virtually all traditional legalisms are unnecessary.

But, you say, how does all this help you, the consumer? You're at the receiving end of all sorts of legal papers—leases, sales contracts, loan notes, warranties, what have you. Will it do you any good if they're written in Plain English?

Yes, it will. The Plain English movement is a consumer movement. Every time a legal document says "pay" instead of "compensation," you gain. Plain English will work in your favor—*if you read it.*

Right now, of course, you *don't* read legal documents. Even if you did, you couldn't understand all the fine points. But you're bound by what you sign or accept.

In this book I've mentioned a few court cases where the consumer won against a corporation that had drafted a contract. (Remember the burglary insurance case?) But those decisions are few and far between—they happen only if a judge considers a certain contract clause outrageous. Otherwise, in the run-of-the-mill case, the consumer is licked from the start. He's signed the paper, hasn't he? Judges go by precedent, the older the more venerable. Over a hundred years ago, the U.S. Supreme Court said (in *Upton v. Tribilcock,* 91 US 45, 50, 1875):

> It will not do for a man to enter into a contract and, when called upon to respond to its obligations, to say that he did not read it when he signed, or did not know what it contained. If this were permitted, contracts would not be worth the paper on which they are written.

This was echoed in a 1961 Kansas case, *Sutherland v. Sutherland* (187 Kan. 599, 358 P. 2nd 776). The defendant was a woman with a verified IQ of 67, whom her own lawyer called an "ignorant moron." Would the court relent? The answer was no:

> A contracting party is under a duty to learn the contents of a written contract before signing it, and if without being a victim of fraud he fails to read the contract or otherwise to learn its contents, he signs the same at his peril and is estopped to deny his obligations thereunder.

So if a contract isn't written in Plain English, you're up against it. You can't read it and, even if you could, there wouldn't be a thing you could do about any features you don't like. True, you can take your business elsewhere, but the other bank loan note or insurance policy will look much the same as the one you refused to sign. The spread of the Plain English movement is your only hope.

So far there have been a number of laws calling for simply written legal documents. For instance, there is the Pension Reform Act that says your employer must give you a simply written booklet explaining his pension or profit-sharing plan. If you're a member of such a plan, *read the booklet.* Study it carefully, look for any options or deadlines, and do what you can to get the most out of it. As long as it's written in Plain English, you owe it to yourself to read it.

Second, there's the Truth in Lending law. It says that all loan notes and retail credit contracts must show you the total finance charge and the annual percentage rate. The total finance charge is the amount the credit will cost you. The annual percentage rate is the rate you'll have to pay. This is the number to compare with what other banks or finance companies offer. For instance, the other day I saw a bank ad that offered a 60-month car loan. It said, "You can borrow $4,400 and pay less than $100 monthly." A table showed that the monthly payment for a $4,400 loan was $99.63. The total finance charge was $1,577.80. The annual percentage rate was 12.79. If you were tempted, you could go to a different bank and see how much *they* charged.

A third field where Plain English must now be used is warranties. From now on you have no excuse if you make a major purchase and don't compare warranties. Read what they offer and *then* make up your mind. One tip: A "full" warranty is almost always better than a "limited" warranty.

Next, there are now a number of states where insurance

policies must be written in Plain English. Some states focus on life insurance policies, some on automobile policies. Most of those laws use a Flesch score as a measure of readability, but it's a watered-down Flesch score. In almost every case, the law as proposed called for a score of at least 60, which means Plain English. By the time the insurance lobbyists had done their work, the minimum score was 40, comparable to the *New York Times* or the *Wall Street Journal*.

Finally, there is the state of New York, whose plain language law went into effect on November 1, 1978. The law doesn't use any formula for measurement, but says consumer contracts must be "written in a clear and coherent manner using words with common and everyday meanings." Other plain language laws are in the works in other states.

You may say these laws won't do anything for the consumer because corporations will simply rewrite their consumer contracts with all the traps and pitfalls still in place. I admit that's possible. In fact, it has already been done by some banks and finance companies. But still, Plain English has tremendous promise for consumers. Let me show you why.

I have in my files two consumer contracts, one a land-sale agreement drafted by a developer, the other a bank loan note. I'll give you a few excerpts from these two documents and translate each into Plain English.

Let's take first the Hillside Acres agreement. (That's not the company's real name, of course.) There's a list of conditions of sale *on the back* of the document. One of them reads:

> **This Agreement constitutes the entire agreement between parties. Purchaser agrees that no representations**

oral or implied have been made to Purchaser to induce him to enter into this Agreement other than those expressly herein set forth.

Plain English translation:

Never mind any promises made by our saiespeople. We're not bound by anything except what's in this contract.

Another clause:

Purchaser may at any time within thirty (30) days hereafter complete a company guided tour of Hillside Acres and request in writing on a form provided by Seller a refund of all monies paid under this Agreement; said form to be executed by Purchaser at Hillside Acres upon completion of tour. The aforesaid is the sole and exclusive procedure for exercising this refund privilege. This refund privilege is personal to the Buyer and cannot be exercised by an Agent on behalf of the Buyer.

Plain English translation:

There's only one way to get a refund of your downpayment. Within 30 days after you've signed this contract, go at your own expense to Hillside Acres and take a guided tour. You must go yourself—don't send anyone else. When you're through with the tour, go to our Hillside Acres sales office. Ask for our official refund request form. A sales agent will be there and try to talk you out of signing it. But if you persist and sign the form, we'll give you your money back.

A third clause:

In the event of failure of Purchaser to pay any installment when due, whether such failure be voluntary or involuntary, the only right of Seller arising thereunder shall be that of termination of this Agreement and retention of all sums previously paid as liquidated damages and not as a penalty, because Seller has taken the property off the real estate market, incurred expenses in selling the property to Purchaser, turned away other prospective purchasers and incurred or will be incurring development and other expenses in connection with the property. Upon such termination, any and all rights Purchaser may have in the property shall immediately terminate and Seller may return the property to its inventory and resell it free and clear of any claims, liens, encumbrances, or defects arising out of this Agreement or Purchaser's rights in the property.

Plain English translation:

If you miss even a single payment, we can cancel this contract and keep all the money you've paid us. You'll lose all your rights.

This gives you a good idea of what you'll find in a typical land sale contract. Now let's move to my bank loan note. (I'll call the bank the Merchants Trust Company.) Again, the note is typical of similar notes now in use all over the country. It's printed on a legal-size sheet of paper, in small type, running close to both margins. The total number of words is 1,714. The average sentence is 57 words long. The readability score on my scale is plus 8—not much better than the Internal Revenue Code.

Here's one clause:

In the event that Merchants Trust shall retain an attorney for the enforcement of the collection of this note, there shall be immediately due from the undersigned, in addition to the unpaid principal and late charges, an attorney's fee of twenty percent of the amounts then owing and unpaid by the undersigned, which the undersigned deems to be reasonable.

Plain English translation:

If we give this note to our lawyers for collection, we'll charge you 20% of the unpaid balance for lawyers' fees. You agree in advance that this is O.K. with you, even if the lawyers send you only a single form letter.

Next clause:

If the undersigned shall default in the punctual payment of any installment or sum payable upon any of, or fail to perform any of the terms and conditions of, said Obligations or the Collateral, or if the conditions or affairs (financial, business or otherwise) of the undersigned shall so change as in the opinion of Merchants Trust to impair its security or increase its credit risk, or if Merchants Trust otherwise deems itself insecure, then and in any such event Merchants Trust may, at its option, declare said Obligations to be immediately due and payable, without notice or demand.

Plain English translation:

Any time we want to, we can declare the whole unpaid balance due at once. We don't have to tell you about it.

Next clause:

The undersigned hereby grants Merchants Trust a security interest in, and pledges, assigns, and transfers to and has deposited with Merchants Trusts or its agents as collateral security for the payment of any and all liabilities and obligations of the undersigned to Merchants Trust and claims of every nature and description of Merchants Trust against the undersigned (including this note and any renewals, extensions, and modifications thereof), whether now existing or hereafter incurred, originally contracts with Merchants Trust and/or with another or others and now or hereafter owing to or acquired by assignment or otherwise, in whole or in part, by Merchants Trust, the following property [blank space for description of collateral].

Plain English translation (let's say the collateral is a car):

You're putting up your car as collateral for this loan. It will also serve as collateral for any other debt you may owe us now or later. For instance, it will serve as collateral for any overdrafts on your checking account.

Next clause:

Merchants Trust may without demand of performance, advertisement or notice of intention to sell, or of the time or place of sale, or to redeem or other notice or demand whatsoever, to or upon the undersigned (all of which are hereby waived), forthwith realize upon, apply or sell, as the case may be, all or any part of said property, at public or private sale, at any exchange, broker's board or at Merchants Trust office or elsewhere, at such prices as it may deem best, for cash, on credit or for future delivery, with the right to Merchants Trust at such sale to purchase all or any part thereof, free from any right or equity of redemption, which right or equity is hereby expressly waived, applying the net proceeds of such realization, application or sale to the payment of said Obligations in such order as Merchants Trust may elect and the undersigned shall remain liable for any deficiency.

Plain English translation:

When we've taken your car, we can sell it to anyone at any price, even to ourselves. We don't have to give you advance notice or a chance to buy it back. We can use the money we get for the car to pay interest, late charges and lawyers' fees first. If the balance doesn't cover your whole debt, you'll still owe us what's left unpaid. You agree in advance that all this will be O.K. with you.

Finally, this clause:

The undersigned also hereby gives Merchants Trust (whether or not any specific collateral is described above) a security interest and a continuing lien for the Obligations in and upon any and all monies, securities and other property of the undersigned and the proceeds thereof, now or hereafter held or received by, or in transit to, Merchants Trust from or for the undersigned, whether for safekeeping, custody, pledge, transmission, collection or otherwise, and also upon any and all deposits (general or special) and credits of the undersigned with, and any and all claims of the undersigned against Merchants Trust, at any time existing.

Plain English translation:

Regardless of any other collateral, all your deposits and credits with us will serve as collateral too. We can at any time take the whole unpaid balance out of your checking or savings account or the contents of your safe deposit box.

I think that all these clauses are what lawyers call unconscionable. What is unconscionable, you ask? I can give you a splendid definition dating back to an English case decided in 1750 (*Earl of Chesterfield v. Janssen,* 2 Ves. Sen. 125, 28 Eng. Rep. 82): "A contract such as no man in his senses and not under delusion would make on the one hand, and as no honest and fair man would accept on the other."

Of course, it's possible that courts will move more and

more to the consumer side and will overrule one such clause after another. But at best this will take many years. In the meantime, Plain English is your best bet.

One day before too long, a customer will walk into a bank and ask for a loan. He'll be given a new, Plain English loan note to sign. He'll sit down, take out his glasses and read the whole note from A to Z. At several places he'll ask questions and get explanations. He'll read about the bank reaching into his checking account, selling his car without telling him, and charging 20 percent of the unpaid loan for a letter on their lawyers' stationery. When he's through, he'll take off his glasses and put them back in his pocket. Then he'll say, "I won't sign this," and walk out.

Index